CREATURE SCENE INVESTIGATION

Loch Ness Monster

FACT OR FICTION?

CREATURE SCENE INVESTIGATION

Loch Ness Monster

FACT OR FICTION?

Rick Emmer

CHELSEA HOUSE PUBLISHERS
An imprint of Infobase Publishing

LOCH NESS MONSTER: FACT OR FICTION?

Copyright © 2010 by Infobase Publishing

All rights reserved. No part of this book may be reproduced or utilized in any form or by any means, electronic or mechanical, including photocopying, recording, or by any information storage or retrieval systems, without permission in writing from the publisher. For information, contact:

Chelsea House
An imprint of Infobase Publishing
132 West 31st Street
New York, NY 10001

Library of Congress Cataloging-in-Publication Data
Emmer, Rick.
  Loch Ness monster: fact or fiction? / by Rick Emmer.
      p. cm. — (Creature scene investigation)
  Includes bibliographical references and index.
  ISBN 978-0-7910-9779-3 (hardcover)
  1. Loch Ness monster—Juvenile literature. I. Title. II. Series.

  QL89.2.L6E66 2010
  001.944—dc22   2009011463

Chelsea House books are available at special discounts when purchased in bulk quantities for businesses, associations, institutions, or sales promotions. Please call our Special Sales Department in New York at (212) 967-8800 or (800) 322-8755.

You can find Chelsea House on the World Wide Web at http://www.chelseahouse.com.

Text design by James Scotto-Lavino, Erik Lindstrom
Cover design by Takeshi Takahashi
Composition by EJB Publishing Services
Cover printed by Bang Printing, Brainerd, MN
Book printed and bound by Bang Printing, Brainerd, MN
Date Printed: January 2010
Printed in the United States of America

10 9 8 7 6 5 4 3 2 1

This book is printed on acid-free paper.

All links and Web addresses were checked and verified to be correct at the time of publication. Because of the dynamic nature of the Web, some addresses and links may have changed since publication and may no longer be valid.

CONTENTS

PREFACE

Welcome to Creature Scene Investigation: The Science of Cryptozoology, the series devoted to the science of **cryptozoology**. Bernard Heuvelmans, a French scientist, invented that word 50 years ago. It is a combination of the words *kryptos* (Greek for "hidden") and *zoology*, the scientific study of animals. So, cryptozoology is the study of "hidden" animals, or **cryptids**, which are animals that some people believe may exist, even though it is not yet proven.

Just how does a person prove that a particular cryptid exists? Dedicated cryptozoologists (the scientists who study cryptozoology) follow a long, two-step process as they search for cryptids. First, they gather as much information about their animal as they can. The most important sources of information are people who live near where the cryptid supposedly lives. These people are most familiar with the animal and the stories about it. So, for example, if cryptozoologists want to find out about the Loch Ness Monster, they must ask the people who live around Loch Ness, a lake in Scotland where the monster was sighted. If they want to learn about Bigfoot, they should talk to people who found its footprints or took its photo.

A cryptozoologist carefully examines all of this information. This is important because it helps the scientist identify and rule out some stories that might be mistakes or lies. The remaining information can then be used to produce a clear scientific description of the cryptid in question. It might even lead to solid proof that the cryptid exists.

Second, a cryptozoologist takes the results of his or her research and goes into the field to look for solid evidence that the cryptid really exists. The best possible evidence would be an actual **specimen**—maybe even a live one. Short of that, a combination of good videos, photographs, footprints, body parts (bones and teeth, for example), and other clues can make a strong case for a cryptid's existence.

In this way, the science of cryptozoology is a lot like **forensics**, the science made famous by all of those crime investigation shows on TV. The goal of forensics detectives is to use the evidence they find to catch a criminal. The goal of cryptozoologists is to catch a cryptid—or at least to find solid evidence that it really exists.

Some cryptids have become world-famous. The most famous ones of all are probably the legendary Loch Ness Monster of Scotland and the apelike Bigfoot of the United States. There are many other cryptids out there, too. At least, some people think so.

This series explores the legends and lore—the facts and the fiction—behind the most popular of all of the cryptids: the gigantic shark known as Megalodon, Kraken the monster squid, an African dinosaur called Mokele-mbembe, the Loch Ness Monster, and Bigfoot. This series also takes a look at some lesser-known but equally fascinating cryptids from around the world:

- the mysterious, blood-sucking Chupacabras, or "goat sucker," from the Caribbean, Mexico, and South America
- the Sucuriju, a giant anaconda snake from South America
- Megalania, the gigantic monitor lizard from Australia
- the Ropen and Kongamato, prehistoric flying reptiles from Africa and the island of New Guinea
- the thylacine, or Tasmanian wolf, from the island of Tasmania

- the Ri, a mermaidlike creature from the waters of New Guinea
- the thunderbird, a giant vulture from western North America

Some cryptids, such as dinosaurs like Mokele-mbembe, are animals already known to science. These animals are thought to have become extinct. Some people, however, believe that these animals are still alive in lands that are difficult for most humans to reach. Other cryptids, such as the giant anaconda snake, are simply unusually large (or, in some cases, unusually small) versions of modern animals. And yet other cryptids, such as the Chupacabras, appear to be animals right out of a science fiction movie, totally unlike anything known to modern science.

As cryptozoologists search for these unusual animals, they keep in mind a couple of slogans. The first is, "If it sounds too good to be true, it probably isn't true." The second is, "Absence of proof is not proof of absence." The meaning of these slogans will become clear as you observe how crypto-zoologists analyze and interpret the evidence they gather in their search for these awesome animals.

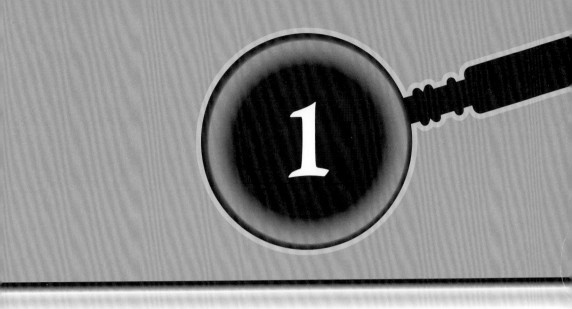

A MONSTER CALLED NESSIE

> Intrigued, I drove up closer, trying to drive and look all at once—and then, incredibly, two or three hundred yards from shore, I saw two sinuous grey humps breaking the surface with seven or eight feet of clear water showing between each. I looked again, blinking my eyes—but there it remained as large as life, lolling on the surface!
>
> —Tim Dinsdale, *Loch Ness Monster*

The British Isles are full of mystery and intrigue. The **peat** bogs of Ireland preserve—in exquisite and grotesque detail—the corpses of people who got stuck in the muck and drowned hundreds of years ago. The ghostly moors of southwestern England provide the perfect setting

The Kelpie was a shape-shifting river monster of Scottish folklore. When disguised as a horse, it would befriend weary travelers and then drown them in the river.

for murder in Sir Arthur Conan Doyle's spine-tingling Sherlock Holmes mystery *The Hound of the Baskervilles*. The most intriguing mystery in all of Britain, however, centers on one particular resident of northern Scotland: the inhabitant of the deep, dark waters of one of the spookiest lakes in the world. The lake goes by the name of Loch Ness (a loch is a Scottish lake), and the beast that is said to live there is one amazing monster.

Scottish folklore is rich with stories about lake and river monsters. Many tales of old are morbid accounts of creatures that made it a point to kill people whenever the opportunity presented itself. The most famous of these was the Kelpie, a shape-shifting spirit that often took the form of a horse that stalked its victims along rivers (hence the Kelpie's other name, Water Horse). When the Kelpie encountered a tired traveler at a river's edge, it would befriend the person, who would eagerly climb on the horse for a restful ride—

whereupon the Kelpie would immediately leap into the river and drown its unsuspecting victim.

The monsters didn't always get their way. According to one ancient legend, St. Columba, an Irish missionary of the Catholic Church, saved a poor man from certain death at the jaws of a water monster inhabiting the River Ness, downstream from the famous loch. The monster had just killed one man and was about to chomp on another when Columba saw the charging beast from the shore. He yelled at the creature in a deep, booming voice, ordering it to back off and leave the man alone. Upon hearing Columba's voice, the monster halted its attack and beat a hasty retreat.

The legend of the Loch Ness Monster is nothing new. Stories about a mysterious beast inhabiting this eerie yet beautiful lake have circulated for centuries. Common sense would tell you that people should have had plenty of time to determine whether the creature is real and, if so, what type of animal it is. Loch Ness is so narrow that you can easily see the opposite shore along its entire length. Yet, true to its cryptid nature, the monster always manages to stay one step ahead of those trying to identify or capture it.

Unlike the bold monsters of old, "Nessie," as the Loch Ness Monster is affectionately called, is a shy, retiring creature that has never harmed a soul. Sure, it has surprised and scared a lot of people, but it has never tried to drown or eat anyone. So it's no surprise that Nessie is one of the most popular of all cryptids, and one of the most perplexing. There have been countless unidentified swimming objects spotted, photographed, filmed, and videotaped in Loch Ness over the years. A person would have to stretch the evidence pretty far, however, just to conclude that Nessie is a real beast of any sort, let alone one sort in particular. (Indeed, some cryptozoologists suspect that Nessie may be nothing more than a figment of overly hopeful imaginations.) Just what is it about

With a length of 24 miles (38 km), a width of one mile (1.6 km), and a depth of more than 800 feet (244 m), Loch Ness is the largest lake in Great Britain. The ruins of Urquhart Castle can be seen in the foreground of this picture.

fabled Loch Ness that enables its famous inhabitant to evade its pursuers time after time?

LOCH NESS: MORE THAN MEETS THE EYE

Loch Ness is a deceptive lake in more ways than one. The water that flows into the loch from surrounding rivers and streams contains a suspension of peat particles that tint the water dark brown and block sunlight from penetrating more than about 13 feet (4 m). What this means is that the vast majority of the water in the loch is never exposed to the light of day or to the eyes of curious residents, tourists, and scientists. It's the perfect place for a shy lake monster to hide.

And while it's certainly true that you can see the opposite shore from practically any vantage point, Loch Ness is hardly what you would call a small lake. In fact, it contains more water than any other lake in Great Britain. While the loch is on average only about one mile (1.6 km) wide, it's about 24 miles (38 km) long. That means the loch has a surface area of about 24 square miles (61 square km). In addition, it's very deep: In some places, the lake bottom plunges to a depth of more than 800 feet (244 m). Because it is so deep, Loch Ness

The Great Glen is a steep-sided, water-filled valley that contains a series of long, narrow lakes, including Loch Ness.

contains an amazing 263 *billion* cubic feet (7.5 billion cubic meters) of water.

The reason that Loch Ness is so long, skinny, and deep is because it is in the Great Glen, a narrow valley that straddles an ancient **fault**, or deep crack, in the Earth's crust. **Erosion** of the edges of the fault over hundreds of millions of years has helped change the original crack into what we see now: a deep, steep-sided valley. Rivers that drain the surrounding countryside keep the valley filled with water, creating a series of long, slender lochs, lined up like a string of sausage links. The largest of the Great Glen lochs, Loch Ness certainly contains more than enough deep, dark water to house and hide a large, aquatic creature.

LET'S GET TECHNICAL: THE GREAT GLEN FAULT

The Great Glen fault slices clear across northern Scotland, from the Atlantic Ocean on the west coast to the North Sea on the east coast. Running in a southwest-to-northeast direction, it is about 60 miles (96 km) long. This fault represents the boundary between two huge slabs of the Earth's **crust**, called **tectonic plates**, which move very slowly across the underlying **mantle**. Over hundreds of millions of years, these two plates have slowly slid past and ground against each other, sometimes generating earthquakes in the process. Earthquakes occur along the Great Glen a few times every century. The most recent one occurred in 2005.

Erosion of the ancient rocky rubble that crumbled to the bottom of the developing valley was given a big boost when an ice age descended upon Scotland about 30,000 years ago. As a huge glacier moved through the valley, it bulldozed most of the debris out of the way. Then, when the ice age ended 10,000 years ago, the great glacier slowly retreated, exposing the scoured-out valley. Having been

Sometimes Nessie almost blows its cover. Every time the beast is spotted, however, it only provides witnesses a tantalizing glimpse that's never clear enough, long enough, or close enough to reveal its true identity. The creature seems to provide just a peek, or perhaps a taunt, to remind people it's still there, waiting to be discovered.

DID YOU SEE THAT?

The year 1933 marked Nessie's debut as a local celebrity. Scottish newspapers had carried little blurbs in the past—interesting but unremarkable sightings of unknown creatures in the loch—but nothing really hooked the public's attention

warped downward under the tremendous weight of the glacier, the Great Glen was initially below sea level and filled with ocean water, forming a channel that connected the Atlantic Ocean to the North Sea. Later, through a process called **isostatic rebound**, Scotland gradually rose above sea level after being relieved of the weight of heavy ice, slowly returning to its pre-ice age height. As a result, the Great Glen was cut off from the ocean, and fresh water from rivers and streams emptied into the Great Glen, flushing out the salt water and creating the freshwater lochs that exist today.

The surface of Loch Ness is now more than 50 feet (15.2 m) above sea level. The northeastern end of Loch Ness drains into the North Sea by means of River Ness. The manmade Caledonian Canal, a system of **locks** (not to be confused with lochs), permits passage of large boats that would otherwise run aground in the shallow River Ness. Another segment of the Caledonian Canal connects the southwest end of Loch Ness with other lochs in the Great Glen and, at the end, the Atlantic Ocean.

until an article titled "A Strange Spectacle on Loch Ness" was published on May 2 in the newspaper *The Inverness Courier*. According to the article, residents John Mackay and his wife

Loch Ness is located in the Scottish Highlands near the town of Inverness. It has become a popular tourist destination, where visitors eagerly hope to catch sight of the fabled creature.

spotted a remarkable animal on the surface of the water as they drove along the road overlooking the north shore of the loch. The description of the scene that unfolded before the Mackays was sure to catch the attention and fire the imagination of anyone reading the story. Spotted three-quarters of a mile (1.2 km) offshore, "the creature disported itself, rolling and plunging for fully a minute, its body resembling that of a whale, and the water cascading and churning like a simmering cauldron. Soon, however, it disappeared in a boiling mass of foam."

The Problem with Eyewitness Accounts

Any good cryptozoologist will tell you that you shouldn't take eyewitness accounts at face value, especially second-hand ones. There could be some details omitted or misrepresented in the telling, resulting in an inaccurate or misleading report. Such is the case with the Mackay story. Months after the article was printed, it was discovered that the Mackays' sighting wasn't that much of a spectacle after all. Because John Mackay was busy driving the car, his wife was the only one who observed it. It was first noticed a mere 100 yards (91 m) away, and the churning water appeared to be caused by two ducks fighting.

So how did one witness turn into two, 100 yards into three-quarters of a mile, and two squabbling ducks into a whalelike beast? The reporter who wrote the article, Alex Campbell, was convinced that an unknown creature inhabited the loch. He may have gone a little overboard in his presentation of the "facts" in order to try to convince nonbelievers that the beast really existed. (Curiously, Campbell himself mistook large waterbirds for the beast on two separate occasions.) There was, however, one item of note to come out of Campbell's story: This was the first time that the unknown creature in the loch was dubbed a "monster," a moniker that has stuck ever since.

Not surprisingly, the Mackay story led to further sightings of Nessie. People familiar with the *Courier* article now kept their eyes peeled for any suspicious monster activity whenever they were in the vicinity of Loch Ness. One of the more interesting of these sightings occurred only two months after the Mackay story was printed. This mid-July sighting was unusual in that it occurred on land, in the middle of the afternoon.

According to this second story, also printed in *The Inverness Courier*, local residents George Spicer and his wife were driving along a road that follows the south shore of the loch when they spotted a "very ugly" creature up ahead, crossing the road. According to the Spicers' original account, the longish, dark gray animal squirted across the road, and they didn't see much detail. No tail was clearly seen, nor a head. It looked, however, as if it might be carrying a small animal in its mouth, perhaps a baby lamb. The size of the animal grew with the telling. At first report, it was about 6.5 feet (2 m) long. After further consideration, it grew to 25 feet (7.6 m), and finally, it maxed out at 29 feet (8.8 m).

If one sticks with the 6.5-foot version of the Spicers' description, the identity of the animal they spotted is not too hard to figure out. It was most certainly an otter. Otters can reach 4 or 5 feet in length, which is in the ballpark of 6.5 feet. (People are notoriously bad at estimating lengths of objects. American Nessie hunter Roy Mackal tested several people for their ability to estimate size and speed of moving unidentified objects and found that they frequently overestimated both measures.)

Otters are agile relatives of the weasel, equally at home on land or in the water, and are known to live in and around Loch Ness. They are primarily dark brown or gray in color, and sometimes carry their young—not lambs—in their mouths. Because few Loch Ness residents were familiar with otters (which, like Nessie, are shy and secretive), the public gobbled up the Spicers' story, and Nessie became the talk of the town—and the subject of many additional sightings. Along with a photograph or two.

Say "Cheese!"

The first photograph of Nessie appeared a few months after the Spicers' story was published. In November 1933, the *Daily Record* newspaper, in Glasgow, Scotland, printed a rather unusual photo of an object in the water. The photographer, Hugh Gray, claimed that his photo showed a large creature that he saw thrashing about in Loch Ness. The photo is blurry and of very poor quality. Although Gray claimed it showed a 40-foot-long (12.2 m) creature with its head submerged and its tail vigorously moving behind, many **skeptics** raised an eyebrow at Gray's explanation. The object in the photo looked a lot like a plain-old tree branch.

One odd feature in Gray's photo is what looks like water spraying into the air along the length of the object. Steuart Campbell, a Nessie skeptic and the author of *The Loch Ness Monster: The Evidence*, notes that it's possible to interpret the blurry object in the photo as nothing more than a rather small branch in the jaws of a swimming dog, in which case the spray could be the result of the dog splashing the branch in the water as it swam to shore. Indeed, the photo is of such poor quality that this explanation is every bit as plausible as Gray's. Since there's no way to verify that the photo was taken at Loch Ness—no shoreline, no horizon, no distinctive landmark of any sort—the object could just as easily be a 4-foot (1.2 m) stick in the mouth of a dog in a backyard pond as it could be a 40-foot monster in the loch. In other words, the photo could easily be a hoax.

CHALLENGES FOR CRYPTOZOOLOGISTS

Cryptozoologists face many challenges as they pursue the Loch Ness Monster. Much of the information they obtain

Photographer Hugh Gray claimed that this picture taken in 1933 showed a 40-foot (12.2 m) monster swimming in Loch Ness. Many people believed that the photo was a hoax.

about Nessie comes from eyewitness accounts. While these stories sometimes provide useful details about the appearance and behavior of an unknown animal, it can be difficult to determine how accurate and truthful the accounts are. In some cases, such as the Mackays' story, the sightings are wildly exaggerated. In others, such as the Spicers' story, the sightings are nothing more than innocent cases of mistaken identity. Sometimes the possibility of a hoax cannot be ruled out, as in the Hugh Gray photograph.

What's more, cryptozoologists themselves make mistakes. (They are human, after all.) Tim Dinsdale, probably the most persistent Nessie hunter during the 1960s, 1970s, and 1980s and author of numerous books about his favorite unknown animal, discovered firsthand how easy it is to

Science writer Steuart Campbell believed that Gray's photo was a blurry picture of a dog swimming with a stick in his mouth. If you look closely at this digitally enhanced version of the previous photograph, you can see the dog's face and the long, curved stick.

be fooled by one's own eyes and expectations. In April 1960, Dinsdale undertook a weeklong stakeout of Loch Ness, hoping to get a glimpse of the beast, and perhaps even film it on his movie camera.

It was on the first day of his expedition, as he was driving along a road bordering the loch, that Dinsdale saw the jaw-dropping, two-humped object described in the quote at the beginning of this section. Elated by his first sighting of Nessie, he slammed on the brakes, hopped out of the car, and hurriedly set up his movie camera, eager to catch Nessie on film. Then, just as he was ready to start filming, he decided to check out those "two sinuous grey humps" through his binoculars before turning on the camera. When viewed through his binoculars, "the humps looked more impressive, larger than life it seemed, and yet when I examined them carefully it was just possible to see a single hairlike twig sprouting out of the one to the right—with a solitary leaf upon it, fluttering gaily in the breeze." Dinsdale's monster was nothing more than a tree trunk. Good trooper that he was, he took his mistake in stride and continued his dogged pursuit of Nessie for more than 25 years.

Now think about this: If someone else had viewed that far-off tree trunk without benefit of binoculars, there might very well have been an article in the next edition of the newspaper, an eyewitness's story about two gray humps splashing about in the middle of Loch Ness—another sighting of the Loch Ness Monster!

No wonder the legend of Nessie continues. Still, one should keep in mind that legends often have a grain of truth behind them. Perhaps that's the case at Loch Ness. Indeed, there's lots of evidence out there that appears to substantiate Nessie's existence. Then again, appearances can be deceiving. With that caution in mind, it is time to begin this creature scene investigation.

INTO THE
LIMELIGHT

During the course of this investigation, some of the most famous—and controversial—cases in Loch Ness Monsterology will be studied. Some alleged Nessie sightings occurred many decades ago, yet they are still unresolved. How can this be? Marion Nestle, a scientist in an entirely unrelated field (she's a **nutritionist**), provided the answer to this question when she recently commented on the controversies that develop within her own area of expertise. Writing in *Scientific American* magazine in 2007, she noted: "Nutrition research is so difficult to conduct that it seldom produces unambiguous results. Ambiguity requires interpretation. And interpretation is influenced by the individual's point of view, which can become thoroughly entangled with the science."

Nestle's observation isn't unique to nutrition science. It applies to other sciences as well, including cryptozoology. Like nutrition research, cryptozoological research is difficult to conduct—if it weren't, unknown animals would not stay unknown for long—and even though all Nessie hunters have the same evidence available to them, each individual weighs the evidence differently. A person who thinks there is a good chance Nessie exists ("After all, those hundreds of eyewitnesses couldn't *all* have been mistaken!") may pay more attention to details that support arguments favoring the existence of the beast. On the other hand, a doubting Thomas ("Let's be reasonable here, no one has captured even *one* specimen, dead or alive, after all these years!") may be more impressed by details that cast doubt on Nessie's existence.

As cryptozoologists pursue Nessie, all they can do is keep gathering and analyzing evidence as carefully and objectively as possible, and be willing to accept the story the evidence tells even if it goes against their hopes and gut feelings. Obviously, this is easier said than done, which is why some Nessie sightings are still the subject of heated debate. But, hey, that's what makes Nessie such a hot topic, and cryptozoology such a cool science.

Let's take a close look at the best of the Nessie evidence.

CASE #1: THE SURGEON'S PHOTO

While the Mackay and Spicer stories and Gray's photo whetted the appetites of monster fans far and wide, Nessie became an even bigger celebrity the next year following the publication of another photographic portrait of the beast. Unlike Gray's photo, this new one was much clearer and showed the silhouette of a typical sea-serpent type of animal: a small head at the end of a long, sinuous neck, sticking high out of the water, periscope-style, as if the monster were surveying the peat-stained waters of its dark domain. Two tiny bumps

This is probably the most famous of all Loch Ness Monster photos. It was submitted to the *Daily Mail* newspaper by Dr. Kenneth Wilson in April 1934.

(horns?) adorned the top of the beast's head, adding a dragon-like touch to the animal's appearance. The photo was reportedly taken by a physician named Kenneth Wilson in early April 1934 and published in the *Daily Mail* newspaper a few weeks later. Dr. Wilson was a respectable physician with an impeccable reputation, so the possibility that the photo was a hoax seemed out of the question. This was definitely the best evidence yet that Nessie really existed.

Nessie hunter Tim Dinsdale was fascinated by Wilson's photograph, which became known as the surgeon's photo.

Dinsdale analyzed the photo long and hard, trying to determine whether it was authentic. Then, all of a sudden, a very
subtle detail in the image jumped out at him: "For a moment
it had no meaning, though now I could see it clearly, and
then its true significance dawned upon me and I realized,
for the first time, with complete assurance, the picture was
not a fake and that the Loch Ness Monster was real. . . . The
picture showed the head and neck of an animal unknown to
science. . . . From this moment of acceptance, my search for
it would begin in deadly earnest!"

Just what was the subtle clue that convinced Dinsdale
that the photo was authentic? In the open water about
14 feet (4.3 m) behind and to the left of Nessie's neck was
a ring of ripples, smaller and much fainter than the ring of
ripples surrounding the beast's neck. Dinsdale figured that a
hoaxer wouldn't have bothered producing a detail so subtle
as to be barely detectable. He therefore decided that those
faint ripples must have been produced by Nessie: The beast's
back end must have just barely broken the surface of the
water and then submerged an instant before Wilson tripped
the shutter on his camera.

Author Peter Costello, another Nessie fan, was equally
impressed with Wilson's photo. In his book *In Search of
Lake Monsters*, he writes: "Seeing how closely the photograph resembles the long-necked aspect of the monster so
often drawn and described—even to those little horns that a
few witnesses have mentioned—can there be any reasonable
doubt that this is a photograph of the Loch Ness animal?"

Not surprisingly, the skeptics among the Nessie hunters
weren't so easily convinced of the authenticity of the surgeon's photo. Roy Mackal, who participated in several Nessie
hunts, was convinced that an unknown animal lurked in the
waters of Loch Ness. He was also convinced that the critter in
this particular photo was not Nessie. He had once mistaken
a large, long-necked waterbird for the beast and believed that

the animal in Wilson's photo was some such bird, perhaps a cormorant or a loon.

Furthermore, in his book *The Monsters of Loch Ness*, Mackal pointed out that the photo Dinsdale analyzed was an enlargement of only a tiny portion (a mere 3%) of the original photo. Dinsdale was therefore unaware that two more ripple rings were visible elsewhere in the original. Mackal thought it was unlikely that all three "extra" sets of ripples could have been produced simultaneously by Nessie's submerged body. They must have had some other source.

Anyone who has closely observed the surface of a lake or fish pond could come up with a number of explanations for a ring of ripples, such as fish nabbing food floating on the water's surface, raindrops, or submerged stones or logs barely breaking the surface as gentle waves flow by. It's doubtful, however, that anything as minor as raindrop ripples could be seen from a distance of 200 to 300 yards (183 to 274 m)—the distance Wilson claimed separated him from the monster. And since the sides of the loch are so steep, there's no way a rock could be breaking the surface that far out from shore, because the water there would be hundreds of feet deep.

Was It All Just a Hoax?

As it turns out, the "monster" in Wilson's photo may not have been all that far from shore, and it may not have been all that big, either: a foot and a half tall at most. In the 1990s, Nessie hunters David Martin and Alastair Boyd dug up the details surrounding the surgeon's photo. According to their findings, the photo was a hoax. Wilson's Nessie wasn't a monster, and it wasn't a loon. According to Martin and Boyd, it was a handmade model stuck on top of a toy submarine.

The story uncovered by Martin and Boyd was full of twists and turns. It began in December 1933, when a fellow by the name of Marmaduke Wetherell was hired by the *Daily Mail* newspaper to lead a search for the lair of the Loch Ness Monster. Wetherell was well known as a big-game hunter, and he loved to be the center of attention. To everyone's surprise, within a few days of the start of his search, Wetherell came across a huge, four-toed footprint along the shoreline of the loch. This was just the sort of sensational story the newspaper was hoping for. A plaster **cast** of the big footprint was sent to the famous British Museum to see what the scientists there could make of it.

Upon finishing their analysis of the cast, the scientists announced their findings to the public: The unusual footprint was identical to that of a hippopotamus—specifically, a hippo's rear left foot. At that point, the credibility of the big-game hunter (you don't suppose he ever bagged a hippo, do you?) and the *Daily Mail* took a nosedive. The newspaper exercised damage control by quietly canceling Wetherell's expedition. Not one more word was written about it.

According to Martin and Boyd, Wetherell didn't like being snubbed by the newspaper, so he decided to get even. His stepson, Christian Spurling, fabricated the monster model and his son, Ian, took a photo of the little toy-submarine-with-a-monster-on-top floating in the shallows near the Loch Ness shore. Kenneth Wilson, who was a bit of a practical joker himself, agreed to submit the photo of Nessie to the *Daily Mail* and claim that he took the picture. He also lied about how he came upon and photographed this large beast swimming in the middle of the loch. The newspaper fell for the hoax and printed Wilson's photo and story—and Wetherell got his revenge.

According to Martin and Boyd, the little Nessie in the Surgeon's photo was only a few yards from the photographer, not hundreds. That means those tiny ripple rings in the photo could indeed be caused by something as ordinary as raindrops or feeding fish, and it means that a tiny, odd-looking object visible right in front of the base of Nessie's neck is probably a part of the little submarine, rather than a weird-shaped little flipper, as hopeful Nessie fans would like to believe.

Further evidence of a hoax surfaced in the form of a second monster photo, which Wilson said he took immediately after he took the first picture. The critter in the second photo, however, didn't look quite like the one in the first picture, and the wave patterns in the second photo looked nothing like those in the first, indicating that the second photo was not taken immediately after the first. It might even have been taken in an entirely different location. The more carefully the evidence was analyzed, the more the details of Wilson's story just didn't add up.

Some die-hard Nessie fans, however, still cling to Wilson's story and argue that Martin and Boyd's story is itself a hoax. The fact of the matter is that without the little "monster sub" in hand (the self-proclaimed perpetrators of the hoax claimed that they sunk it in the loch), no one can really prove that the story Martin and Boyd uncovered is true. There is now, however, enough reason to doubt the authenticity of the surgeon's photo that this picture no longer enjoys the respect it once commanded—especially since Wilson reportedly claimed to have taken his famous photos on the first day of April. That's right: April Fools' Day!

CASE #2: THE DINSDALE FILM

When Tim Dinsdale undertook his April 1960 expedition to Loch Ness, the image of the surgeon's photo was still untarnished, and he was convinced that the unknown beast in the photo inhabited the loch. So even though his first sighting turned out to be a case of mistaken identity, he continued his search in earnest. He was finally rewarded with another sighting.

On the morning of the last day of his expedition, April 23, Dinsdale was driving along the south shore of Loch Ness. His movie camera, loaded with black-and-white film and mounted on a tripod, sat on the seat beside him, ready for action. While passing a clearing in the trees overlooking a scenic bay, Dinsdale noticed an object far out in the loch. The object looked a bit shorter than the 15-foot (4.6 m) fishing boats commonly seen in the loch, and when he viewed the object through binoculars, he thought it sat higher in the water than a fishing boat. He also noticed that it had a distinct reddish-brown color, with a darker blotch on its side.

Dinsdale eagerly turned on his movie camera and filmed the object as it zigzagged its way toward the north shore. Before it reached the shore, the object appeared to submerge momentarily as it turned to the left and moved parallel to the shore, moving at a speed of about 10 miles per hour (16 km per hour). Although the object was just a small spot in the camera viewfinder, Dinsdale could easily see a V-shaped **wake** or wave pattern fanning out to the sides behind the object as it moved through the water. He also saw "rhythmic bursts of foam" break the surface at the side of the object as it moved forward. To Dinsdale, it was obvious that these foam bursts were caused by flipper strokes—strokes made by a swimming monster.

Running low on film (he had exposed most of it earlier that week), Dinsdale decided to try to get closer to the beast for his final shoot. He stopped the camera, sped down the road to a better vantage point, and searched for the monster, but by then it had apparently disappeared into the dark depths of the loch. Still, Dinsdale was exhilarated, because he was convinced he had finally caught the Loch Ness Monster in action on film. "Through the magic lens of my camera I had reached out, across a thousand yards and more, to *grasp the monster by the tail,*" he wrote in his book *Loch Ness Monster.*

Later that morning, Dinsdale filmed a reenactment of the beast's morning swim, using the one object most likely to be mistaken for the animal: a small boat. Dinsdale filmed a local resident who guided a boat along the same route his Nessie had followed that morning. Subsequent analysis of the two films showed that the animal and the fishing boat looked nothing alike. The animal, when visible, looked like an indistinct blob, whereas the boat looked like, well, a boat. The two objects' wakes were distinct as well. While both objects created visible V-wakes as they plowed through the water, the outboard motor at the rear of the boat produced a very noticeable wake of its own, a result of the propeller churning up the water at the surface of the loch. This propeller wake looked like a long tail extending from the back of the boat, splitting the V-wake down the middle. No obvious "tail wake" was visible behind Dinsdale's Monster.

A few years later, the now-famous Dinsdale film was analyzed by photo experts at the Joint Air Reconnaissance Intelligence Center of Britain's Royal Air Force. JARIC concluded that the object in the film was "probably an animate object." Dinsdale was understandably ecstatic at this conclusion and became totally convinced that the object he filmed that April morning was the one and only Loch Ness Monster. With such powerful **corroboration** of Dinsdale's story by a prestigious branch of the British armed forces, it is no surprise that this famous film—all four minutes of it—stood for decades as the strongest evidence yet for the existence of Nessie.

Another Case of Mistaken Identity

Not everyone was convinced that Dinsdale's film was so fascinating. According to Steuart Campbell, the difference between the wakes produced by Dinsdale's beast and the little boat was one of degree, not of kind. That is, both objects produced V-wakes typically produced by boats. Careful study of the Dinsdale film showed that the alleged beast also produced a wake just like a boat's propeller wake, but it was extremely faint and easy to overlook. In Campbell's opinion, the difference in the appearance of the wakes produced by the two objects was simply due to different light and water surface conditions prevailing during the early morning filming of Dinsdale's Monster and the midmorning filming of the boat.

LET'S GET TECHNICAL: BOAT WAKES

*W*aves are interesting, dynamic features of any large body of water. They appear almost alive as they move along the surface and lap against the shore. Some waves, particularly those produced by moving objects (such as boats and swimming animals), have properties that bear directly on the study of the Loch Ness Monster, so it's important to understand the behavior of these natural phenomena in order to effectively study sightings of Nessie.

A wave produced by an object moving in the water is called a wake. A moving boat produces a V-shaped wake as it cuts through the water, pushing the water in front of it to the sides as it advances. This V-wake is composed of two waves that spread out behind the boat, creating the two arms of the "V."

You can easily demonstrate a miniature version of a boat wake by trailing your finger along the surface of the water in a bathtub. Your moving finger forms the point of the V, from which the wake grows and spreads out behind. Eventually, the two arms of the wake will reach the sides of the tub. There, they will bounce, or reflect, off the sides and head back toward the middle of the tub.

Because Loch Ness has such steep, rocky sides, it acts almost like a giant bathtub, reflecting boat wakes back toward the center

Now, what about the fact that the object briefly submerged? Obviously, a fishing boat wouldn't do that, but a swimming animal surely could. According to the JARIC report, the apparent submergence of the object could have been an optical illusion caused by peculiar light conditions existing at the moment of filming. In other words, the object could have been afloat the whole time. It could have been a boat after all.

In 1984, nearly a quarter of a century after that fateful day in the life of Tim Dinsdale, the identity of the object

of the lake. When these reflected wakes collide with each other, things really get interesting. When waves collide, they interact with each other in a process called **interference**. They actually pass right through each other, but as they do so, they combine to create a bigger wave that looks as if a large, hump-shaped object is rising to the surface.

When wakes from all the boats traveling up and down the loch collide with each other, with their reflections off the sides of the loch, and with waves generated by the wind, all sorts of complicated interference patterns can develop. These patterns often form several minutes after all passing boats have left the area. They may develop into one or more humps, of equal or varying size, located at various distances from each other, but often of the same size and in line with each other. These interference wave patterns may move, sometimes at a high rate of speed, or they may remain in place, forming **standing waves**.

Interference wave patterns do indeed seem to have a life of their own when they rise, move, hover, and flatten out as their component waves interact with each other. Over the years, many sightings of such waves have undoubtedly been mistaken for Nessie.

in the film was determined beyond all reasonable doubt. While viewing a videotaped copy of the film, Nessie hunters Adrian Shine, Ricky Gardiner, and Tony Harmsworth studied the film while the video controls were set for extra-high contrast. When viewed in this manner, the faint shape of a small boat and its single human occupant stood out from the background water. When viewed under normal contrast, the boat, its occupant, and the water in the background were all nearly the same shade of gray (remember, this movie was in black and white, not color), and the boat and person blended in so well with the water as to become invisible.

The results were clear: Dinsdale's Nessie was just a fishing boat. Dinsdale, however, never learned of the results of this video analysis. Because he was extremely ill when Shine and the others made their discovery, they respectfully waited until after his death in 1987 to publicize their findings.

As cases 1 and 2 show, the best above-water photographic evidence (the surgeon's photo) and motion-picture evidence (the Dinsdale film) for Nessie fizzled out when persistent Nessie hunters maintained their search for, and finally discovered, the truth. There's other evidence out there, however. Other strategies have been employed by Nessie chasers in more recent times, utilizing modern, high-tech equipment. Unlike earlier attempts to find Nessie, the more recent ones have taken the search to Nessie's own domain: the dark water beneath the surface of Loch Ness.

As the next chapter will show, these underwater searches have produced results that are both tantalizing and controversial. It's time for us to descend into the deep, dark depths of Loch Ness and see what the fuss is all about.

SEARCHING
BENEATH THE
SURFACE

*I*n the 1960s, the surgeon's photo and Tim Dinsdale's motion picture were still regarded by many Nessie hunters as strong evidence for the existence of at least one large, unknown beast in Loch Ness. In fact, the Dinsdale film was so convincing to Nessie fans that an official Nessie-hunting organization, the Loch Ness Phenomena Investigation Bureau (LNPIB), was established in 1962. Later renamed the Loch Ness Investigation Bureau (LNIB), the organization conducted annual Nessie searches for the next decade, until it disbanded in late 1972.

The LNIB's expeditions became more elaborate with each passing year, utilizing high-tech equipment, and culminating

In 1969, the one-man submarine *Viperfish*, armed with two tissue-sampling harpoons, was used to hunt for Nessie. The hunt came up empty.

in the use of mini-submarines in 1969. The first sub to be launched in the Nessie search was the *Viperfish*, a one-man sub that was armed with harpoon guns mounted on the sub's snout. These guns were loaded with special tissue-sampling devices which, if deployed, would have poked into Nessie's skin and snipped out a small piece of flesh. The flesh could be retrieved and taken to a lab for analysis. Such a tissue sample might tell researchers what type of animal the beast was: fish, reptile, whale, or whatever.

Unfortunately, the *Viperfish* never made contact with any monsters. It did, however, make contact with the bottom of Loch Ness. On its first descent, the sub plowed into the muck at the bottom of the loch and got stuck. Fortunately, sub operator Dan Taylor was able to free the *Viperfish* from the grip of the loch bottom.

The next submarine to tackle Loch Ness was the larger *Pisces*, a six-man sub that was equipped with **sonar** to search for large objects—such as lake monsters—that might be moving about in the depths of the loch. On one occasion, the sonar detected a large moving object, but whatever the object was, it took off when the *Pisces* approached to within about 100 yards (91 m).

Although no definitive results were obtained from these adventures, the sonar "hits" obtained by the *Pisces* and in other experiments indicated that sonar could be a valuable tool in the search for Nessie. Apparent proof that this was the case would soon materialize in a joint sonar/underwater photography expedition that produced some of the most exciting Nessie evidence of all time: the famous "flipper" photos.

CASE #3: THE FLIPPER PHOTOS

In August 1972, an American made a big splash in the hunt for the Loch Ness Monster. Robert Rines, founder and director of the Academy of Applied Science in Boston, Massachusetts, spearheaded a joint Nessie hunt with the LNIB. This was a high-tech venture, involving a clever setup that coordinated sonar with underwater flash photography. Rines's plan was to plant a sonar unit and an underwater camera, equipped with a powerful flash unit, on the bottom of the loch. By positioning the sonar above and behind the camera, as if looking over the camera's shoulder, the researchers hoped to obtain simultaneous sonar and photo evidence for any large moving object—hopefully Nessie—that passed in front of the camera.

From the research boat *Narwhal*, the sonar unit was carefully lowered by cable until it reached a point on the loch floor, 35 feet (10.7 m) down. The camera was positioned in deeper water, some 120 feet (36.6 m) ahead of the sonar, by a second boat, the *Nan*. The sonar ran continuously, and the camera was rigged to take a flash photo every 55 seconds.

Success!

In the pitch-black early morning hours of August 8, the researchers hit pay dirt. Two large blobs appeared briefly on the sonar display, and the camera took several pictures

---

LET'S GET TECHNICAL: SONAR

Sonar (*sound navigation and ranging*) is a versatile instrument that uses sound waves to detect objects under water. Sound waves travel through water better than light waves, especially in the peat-stained water of Loch Ness. So sonar would seem to be the perfect tool to use in finding and tracking large animals moving about in the black depths of the loch.

A sonar unit consists of three major components: a **transmitter**, a **receiver**, and a **display**. The transmitter emits a brief pulse of sound, called a **ping**, at regular intervals. If a ping encounters an object in the water, it bounces off the object, creating an **echo**. The echo is detected by the receiver and then displayed on a computer monitor or some other device.

Unfortunately, because sound waves are much longer than light waves, sonar cannot produce an image as sharp as can be obtained from a camera. Sonar images typically appear as irregular blotches on the display. Although the exact shape of the object cannot be determined, the size of the blotch does give a rough idea of the size of the object.

Furthermore, sonar can determine the **range** of the reflecting object—that is, how far away it is. This is done by multiplying the speed of sound in water (1 mile [1.6 km] per second) by the time elapsed between the transmission of the ping and the reception of

before the blobs disappeared. When the camera film was later developed, a few frames (reportedly corresponding to the time interval when the blob was displayed on sonar) showed a couple of objects of some sort in front of the camera. However, the news was not all good: Because the peaty water scattered the light from the flash unit (an effect similar to shining a flashlight in a thick fog), the pictures were very bright, very blurry, and, unfortunately, lacking in detail.

the echo. This value is divided by two, because the ping only took half of the total time to reach the object; the echo took the other half to bounce back to the receiver.

For example, if the elapsed time between ping transmission and echo reception was 0.6 seconds, the range of the object would be calculated as follows:

$$\text{object range} = \frac{(\text{speed of sound}) \times (\text{total elapsed time})}{2}$$

$$= \frac{(1 \text{ mile per second}) \times (0.6 \text{ seconds})}{2}$$

$$= 0.3 \text{ mile } (0.5 \text{ km})$$

The submarine *Pisces* was able to achieve a much smaller range than this—a mere 100 yards—as it approached the large, unidentified object it detected while searching for Nessie. Still, this football-field distance was not close enough to allow visual contact. As the sub tried to approach even closer, a sudden increase in the elapsed time between ping transmission and echo reception indicated that the invisible target had moved away. Close, but no cigar!

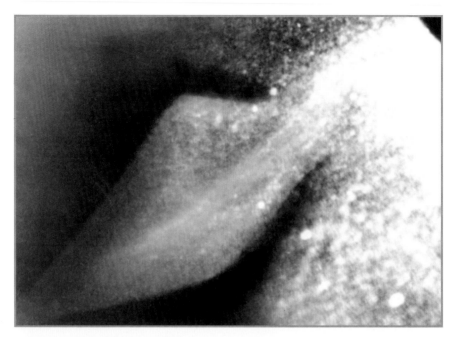

This is the published version of one of the famous "flipper" photos, taken in 1972 during Robert Rines's Loch Ness expedition. The image was produced by a strobe-equipped underwater camera.

In order to get a better view of the objects in the photos, Rines sent the pictures to the NASA Jet Propulsion Laboratory in California for computer enhancement. During this process, a blurry image is made clearer by adjusting the contrast of the different shades of color in the image, a process that "lifts the fog," making edges and other details of objects in the photo easier to see.

The results of computer enhancement of two of Rines's photos were mindboggling. Both images showed what looked like a diamond-shaped flipper of a huge animal. Mathematical calculations determined that the flipper was about 6.5 feet (2 m) long. The flipper in the second image, presumably the same one as in the first image, was posed at a slightly different angle, meaning that it had moved. This strongly suggested that a huge animal with 6.5-foot-long flippers had swum in front of the camera. Rines was ecstatic. Here at last were solid photographic and sonar evidence suggesting that a huge unknown beast inhabited Loch Ness!

As spectacularly successful as this Loch Ness expedition appeared to be, no one would have expected Rines to achieve equal success on any future venture, but achieve it he did. Three years later, Rines's second underwater expedition appeared to capture on film a close-up of the one body part of the monster that would be even more impressive than a flipper: the head—in all its hideous glory.

CASE #4: THE "GARGOYLES'S HEAD"

Rines's 1975 expedition was another combined sonar/photo venture. This time around, the sonar did not record anything significant, but the camera certainly did. Three photos showed uninteresting bottom debris. One photo, however, showed a blurry image of what looked like a large-bodied, stubby-flippered beast with a small head perched at the end of a long neck. The head and neck looked somewhat like those of the critter in the surgeon's photo, which was still held in high regard because Wetherell's hoax had not yet been revealed. Another photo showed an object that author and Nessie hunter Henry Bauer described as looking vaguely like the head and neck of a crocodile.

The most interesting photo of all showed what looked like a massive head, complete with paired horns and eyes, and a broad snout—the very essence of a monster. This object appeared to exhibit **bilateral symmetry**. Such symmetry, where the left side is a mirror image of the right side, is typical of most animals. Such symmetry, however, is almost unheard of in objects such as rocks or tree stumps, the only other objects that this "Gargoyle's head," as the object was nicknamed, could possibly be.

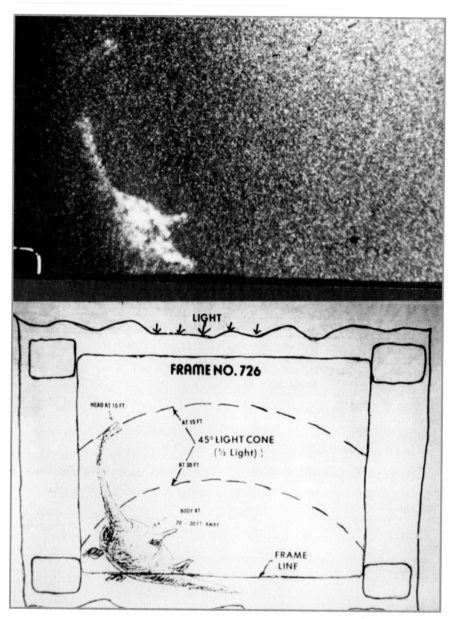

Taken during Robert Rines's 1975 expedition, this photograph appears to show the torso, neck, and head of an underwater creature. The drawing beneath the photograph is a scientist's notes on how the light entered the water and illuminated the animal's head and body.

Rines was so convinced he had discovered an animal species new to science that he and a fellow Nessie hunter, LNIB director Sir Peter Scott, held a news conference to announce that they had given Nessie an official scientific name, *Nessiteras rhombopteryx*, meaning "Ness monster with rhomboidal fin." (A **rhomboid** is a diamond-shaped geometrical figure.)

Still, the skeptics weren't convinced. Many scientists, including several Nessie-hunting cryptozoologists, weren't so eager to accept Rines's evidence as proof that a monstrous cryptid inhabited Loch Ness. They examined all of the photo and sonar evidence in painstaking detail, and the harder they looked, the more Rines's case appeared to crumble.

Seeing Isn't Always Believing

There was a problem with the flipper photos. Although the computer enhancement technique used on Rines's photos at the Jet Propulsion Laboratory was a perfectly legitimate process used to "clean up" blurry photographs, the JPL's results looked nothing like the final images that were published in magazines and newspapers. In fact, the JPL photos were still pretty fuzzy and hard to interpret. The published photos, on the other hand, had apparently been by retouched by an artist, so that a diamond-shaped flipper clearly stood out from the background. Someone had fiddled with the flippers! No one from Rines's group had mentioned that fact when the photos were published. Suggestions of tampering with the evidence, sloppy scientific methods, and the like soon surfaced, and a war of words broke out between Rines's camp and the skeptics. To this day, the controversy around the flipper photos still surfaces from time to time. The sonar results from the 1972 expedition haven't fared any better.

This is the actual computer-enhanced version of one of Robert Rines's flipper photos. It does not look as flipperlike as the version published by Rines.

A Case of Wishful Thinking

Nutritionist Marion Nestle's comment about controversy in science hit the nail of the Nessie controversy right on the head. In analyzing the 1972 sonar results, Rines and his sonar experts appeared to have let their pro-Nessie point of view become entangled with their interpretation of the data. They saw in the sonar display what they expected to be there (a couple of huge beasts with humped backs and flippers), not what was actually there (a couple of big, indistinct blobs, one of which was bordered by a couple of faint wavy patterns). By concentrating only on those exciting blobs, the experts failed to notice—or at least to mention—a very important clue in the sonar readout: an echo reflecting off the bottom of the loch. This echo kept changing range. Now unless the bottom of the loch were moving to and fro on that August night, the only explanation for this phenomenon was that the sonar unit itself was moving around. This movement could be caused either by the tether cable connecting the sonar to the *Narwhal* being tugged this way and that by water currents, or by the boat itself being jostled by the wind.

According to Tony Harmsworth, Webmaster for the Loch Ness Information Site, the fact that the sonar unit was moving is extremely important. It means that the sonar could have been pointing in practically any direction, including up toward the surface of the loch. In fact, wavy sonar readings such as those Rines recorded are typical of surface wave and boat wake echoes. Therefore, a very plausible explanation for the blob with the wavy lines on the sonar display is that the sonar was pointing toward the surface and receiving echoes bouncing off surface waves and the bottom of one of the research boats. Because this was a distinct possibility, Rines's sonar results did nothing to corroborate the story behind the flipper photos.

To make matters worse, since Rines's sonar unit was moving around, it's quite possible that his camera was also moving around and, at some point, angled downward. If such were the case, the objects it photographed could quite easily have been nothing more than nearby debris resting on the bottom of the loch.

What about the later photos of the "Gargoyle's head," the crocodile's head, and the long-necked beast with the tiny head? As Henry Bauer noted, "If there are no Nessies, what are the chances that 3 out of 6 underwater photographs . . . would capture logs or debris that look like various parts of a Nessie?" As it turns out, the chances for the "Gargoyle's head" were pretty good.

In 1987, during a venture sponsored by the Loch Ness Project, Nessie hunter Dick Raynor found the "Gargoyle's head" on the floor of the loch with the help of an underwater video camera. The grotesque apparition was nothing more than a weathered, waterlogged tree stump. If one of the three objects was definitely proven to be a tree stump, then it's certainly possible, even likely, that the other two objects were also simply tree stumps, logs, or other bottom debris. That would go a long way toward explaining why the "heads" of the objects in the three photographs all looked different—a difficult detail to explain, unless one assumes Nessie to be an accomplished shape-shifter like its Kelpie predecessors.

All in all, Rines's photos turned out to be a bust. No one has come up with any better underwater photo evidence in the years since Rines's 1975 effort. So it is not surprising that many Nessie hunters believe—despite the questionable initial interpretation of Rines's 1972 sonar results—that if Nessie really exists in the deep, dark, peaty waters of Loch Ness, it's more likely to be detected by sonar than by camera.

One of the most famous of all Loch Ness sonar searches was conducted in 1987 by the same people who discovered that famous gargoyle tree stump. In the days leading up to this high-profile event, many Nessie fans were optimistic that their quarry would finally be flushed out of hiding. The results were not what they had hoped for.

CASE #5: OPERATION DEEPSCAN

In October 1987, Loch Ness Project director Adrian Shine led a massive, coordinated search for Nessie. Using a whole fleet of boats equipped with sophisticated sonar systems, Shine's Operation Deepscan systematically searched Loch Ness from end to end, looking for signs of the beast.

The search was conducted with military precision. On the morning of October 9, near the northeast end of the loch, a flotilla of 19 boats lined up side-by-side, spanning nearly the entire width of the loch. As each boat was equipped with its own sonar unit, the flotilla formed one big sonar "net" that swept almost completely across the narrow loch as the line of boats slowly cruised to the southwest end of the loch. Whenever an **anomaly**—Nessie?—was detected, sonar-equipped chase boats behind the flotilla quickly zoomed over and tried to home in on the object and track its movements. The next morning, the flotilla reversed direction and repeated the sweep as it made its way back to the northeast end.

On the first day of Operation Deepscan, the flotilla detected three anomalies, ranging in depth from 256 to 571 feet (78 to 174 m). Unfortunately, none of the chase boats found anything. The sonar sweep the next day was also unsuccessful. Despite all the hoopla surrounding Operation Deepscan, the results of the sonar sweeps were disappointing. Shine was unable to identify the anomalies. He thought that they might have been nothing more than false hits created by the numerous ping echoes of the flotilla's sonar units.

False echoes are not the only source of unidentifiable sonar anomalies. Shine believes that some of these anomalies are caused by **turbulence**: Something stirs up the water, but it's impossible to determine what that something is. Evidence like this is tantalizing—perhaps the turbulence was caused by a Nessie that splashed by just moments before—but by itself it proves nothing.

So Far, Not So Good

Operation Deepscan was not the only significant sonar search performed at Loch Ness. As long ago as 1962, personnel from Cambridge University executed a sonar sweep similar to Operation Deepscan. No anomalies were detected during

In 1987, a flotilla of sonar-equipped search boats swept Loch Ness, looking for signs of Nessie. This expedition, known as Operation Deepscan, produced no conclusive evidence for the existence of the creature.

this sweep. A 1968 sonar search, however, led by D.G. Tucker of the University of Birmingham detected as many as eight large objects moving around at a depth of as much as 656 feet (200 m), nearly at the bottom of the loch. Unfortunately, the identity of the objects could not be pinned down. In 1969, Nessie hunter Robert Love, cruising Loch Ness with his sonar-equipped boat, detected what may have been a large animal at a depth of 220 feet (67 m). It slowly moved in a big loop a few hundred yards away and then moved out of sonar range.

In 1983, sonar experts Rikki Razdan and Alan Kielar set up 144 individual floating sonar units spread out over a relatively small 82-by-82-foot (25-by-25-m) square on the surface of Loch Ness, located in an area where numerous eyewitness sightings of Nessie had been reported. Razdan and Kielar monitored their sonar array for seven weeks, during which time nothing larger than a 3.3-foot (1-m) fish was detected.

Robert Rines, never a quitter, returned to Loch Ness a number of times after he photographed the "Gargoyle's head" in 1975. His most notable sonar search for Nessie occurred in 2001 when his research boat swept the whole length of Loch Ness eight times. The result? According to Rines, "No large mid-water targets were detected."

Finally, in 2003, the British Broadcasting Corporation sponsored a sonar sweep of Loch Ness that used "600 separate sonar beams and satellite navigation technology to ensure that none of the loch was missed." The result? Again, no sign of Nessie.

MOVING ON

It's time to take stock of the situation. What evidence do we have? We've just presented the strongest cases to date in the search for Nessie. We've shown that the surgeon's photo is most likely a hoax. Tim Dinsdale's film—long regarded as the best evidence of all—was shown to be a case of mistaken identity. Robert Rines's photo and sonar evidence from the 1970s is of dubious value at best. Operation Deepscan detected no beast. Other sonar searches have either come up empty or detected objects that might be unknown creatures, but might also be ordinary known inhabitants of Loch Ness, such as fish. That's not much evidence to go on: an assortment of unexplained sonar anomalies. That, plus a whole slew of eyewitness accounts, which, as previously demonstrated, are not always accurate.

The best thing to do at this point is to consider all the possible candidates for the title of Loch Ness Monster and see which one(s), if any, fit the bits and pieces of evidence that have come to light. As it turns out, there's a whole boatload of possibilities.

THE
CANDIDATES

*W*hat's big and brown, and has a long neck, a small head, flippers, horns, humps, a mane, and a tail? Nessie, of course. Nessie witnesses often include most and sometimes all of these features when they describe the creature they think they saw swimming in Loch Ness. Because no known creature has all of these features, many people feel that Nessie must be a bizarre creature unknown to modern science. That, however, is not necessarily the case. When eyewitness accounts are carefully examined, it is often possible to tell just exactly what it was that an observer saw. It wasn't a monster or sea serpent. Sometimes it wasn't even alive.

As previously mentioned, many Nessie sightings are actually sightings of wave- and wake-interference patterns. Other nonliving Nessie sightings have been attributed to floating logs (such as the one that fooled Tim Dinsdale). A log can actually behave like a live animal. Under certain conditions, water near the surface of Loch Ness actually flows into the wind, against the waves. "When this happens," says Adrian Shine, "objects on the surface such as logs can be borne along against the wind looking just like swimming animals." A 30-foot (9.1-m) log can turn into a 30-foot monster.

Many other sightings have been attributed to animals. Over the years, many beasts have been nominated as the creature most likely to be Nessie. Everything from a prehistoric whale to an overgrown salamander to a gigantic version of a bizarre, long-extinct wormlike creature has had its moment in the spotlight at one time or another. It's really not necessary, however, to invoke such far-out explanations for the majority of sightings.

BIRDS OF A FEATHER

Waterbirds have been the focus of a number of Nessie "sightings." If you picture in your mind the silhouette of the object in the surgeon's photo, you'll probably picture a humplike body behind a long, graceful neck and head that arc high out of the water. Many waterbirds have exactly that swanlike appearance when viewed in profile. Mergansers (diving, fish-eating ducks), loons, and cormorants are not uncommon visitors to Loch Ness. These diving birds are excellent swimmers capable of chasing their fish prey under water, sometimes at a considerable depth. Many reports of long-necked Nessies sinking or plunging into the water have been attributed to such birds diving for food. According to Steuart Campbell, however, "the deception is most marked when the birds take off and fly close to the water, beating the surface with their wing tips. They become a series of humps, shrouded in spray, speeding across the water and leaving behind them a wake much larger than one would expect."

The cormorant is a large waterbird that has sometimes been mistaken for the Loch Ness Monster.

How can a duck- or goose-sized waterbird possibly be mistaken for a huge beast? In some cases, the eyewitnesses may simply have let their imaginations go wild. In other cases, however, the animal sighted really was super-sized—in a way. Recall that Alex Campbell twice mistakenly identified waterbirds as Nessie. His two sightings were about a month apart, and it wasn't until the second sighting that he realized that *both* sightings were cases of mistaken identity. In a letter he wrote several weeks after his first encounter with "Nessie," he explained:

> Last Friday I was watching the Loch at the same place and about the same time of day [as the first sighting].

The weather was almost identical—practically calm and the sun shining through a hazy kind of mist. . . . I discovered that what I took to be the monster was nothing more than a few cormorants, and what seemed to be the head was a cormorant standing in the water and flapping its wings . . . The bodies of the birds were magnified out of all proportion. . . . This miragelike effect I have often seen on Loch Ness . . . it gives every object—from, say, a gull or a bottle to an empty barrel—a very grotesque appearance provided that such objects are far enough away.

A mirage? Over a lake? That's right. Mirages aren't found only in deserts. Under the right atmospheric conditions, a mirage can materialize just about anywhere. If it appears at Loch Ness, a bird can change into a huge monster.

IT'S OTTERLY AMAZING

Birds don't have a monopoly on Nessie look-alikes. Mammals also have fooled many observers into thinking they saw a monster in the loch.

The Spicers' account, previously described, is a perfect example of a Nessie sighting with a mammalian twist. George Spicer had no clue as to the identity of the awesome beast he saw. In a letter he wrote to a newspaper, he described the long-necked, hump-backed creature he spotted crossing the road as "the nearest approach to a dragon or pre-historic animal that I have ever seen in my life." Yet, the details he provided made it quite clear to anyone familiar with the **fauna** of the Loch Ness area that Spicer's dragon was nothing more than an otter.

Otters are undoubtedly responsible for lots of Nessie sightings, and it's easy to see why. Otters are agile critters, and in the water they are really in their element. They can easily swim 7 mph (11.2 km per hour), which equals or exceeds the speeds reported for many swimming Nessies. An otter can tread water, thrusting its head and long neck a foot or more straight up out of the water, in a way reminiscent of the pose of the creature in the surgeon's photo. An otter can also make quite a commotion at the surface when chasing fish or playing with a family member. (Otters are very sociable

LET'S GET TECHNICAL: MIRAGES

The shimmering "lake" seen hovering over hot pavement or baking desert sand may be the most well-known mirage, but it is far from the most amazing. Mirages over water can produce some pretty far-out optical illusions, including visions of spectacular lake monsters such as Nessie.

Many Nessie sightings are made during "Nessie weather," the quiet, windless early-morning calm that envelops Loch Ness during much of the year. Because the loch water is so cold, air that settles on the water overnight may become much cooler than the air above it, creating what is known as a **temperature inversion**. The cold bottom layer of the temperature inversion works like a magnifying lens, bending or **refracting** light rays near the horizon in such a way as to make objects appear much bigger and closer than they really are.

Because cold air is denser than warm air, a temperature inversion over the waters of Loch Ness is a stable situation. As the sun rises and breezes develop, however, the cool air and the warm air eventually mix together, causing the temperature inversion to break up. During this mixing process, the magnified objects in a mirage will be seen to shimmer, move around, or bob up and down at the surface. This makes it easy to understand how a distant otter or waterbird, swimming on the horizon and kicking up a wake behind it, can look like a big, long, swan-necked Loch Ness Monster.

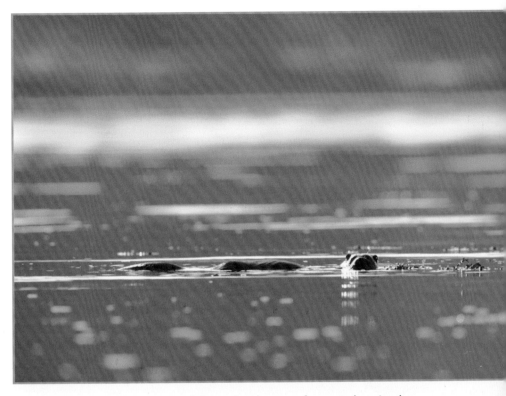

The European otter is one of the animals most frequently mistaken for Nessie.

animals; parents and pups live as a family unit until the young are able to fend for themselves.)

Furthermore, when an otter family goes for a swim, it is not uncommon for the animals to line up single file, as if playing follow-the-leader. A distant observer could easily mistake the line of otters for a single, very long, multi-humped, serpentlike Nessie.

OH, DEER!

Otters aren't the only mammals that have been mistaken for Nessie. One mammal is a beautiful, stately animal that

Roe deer occasionally swim across Loch Ness. If seen in the dim light of dawn or dusk, they may be mistaken for the Loch Ness Monster.

would seem the most unlikely creature to be mistaken for a monster from the deep.

In 1952, Greta Finlay and her young son were walking along the shore of Loch Ness when they were startled by what they thought was a horned monster swimming in the loch a short distance away. The boy later drew a picture of the beast. It had a head adorned with short, knobby horns, perched atop an upright neck (recall the surgeon's photo), behind which two humps stuck out of the water. If one weren't familiar with the wildlife of the Loch Ness area, such a creature might indeed appear unusual, even downright scary. To people in the know, however, the animal in the boy's picture was nothing to fear. It was a deer—specifically, a male roe deer, a small deer common to much of Europe, including the Scottish highlands surrounding Loch Ness.

The reddish-brown to black roe deer stands about 30 inches (76 cm) tall and is only a bit over 4 feet (1.2 m) long, so one would hardly think that such an animal—a land animal, at that—could be mistaken for a water monster. Consider, however, these facts: Young roe bucks (male deer) sprout tiny, knobby antlers that only grow a few inches high; roe deer are good swimmers and have been known to swim across the loch; roe deer swim low in the water, so there is a considerable gap of open water between the neck and the rump, which looks like a hump rising out of the water; and the wake the swimming deer leaves behind can create the appearance of a second hump. It's easy to see how a swimming roe deer might be mistaken for a two-humped, horned monster, especially in the dim light of dawn or dusk, which is when the **crepuscular** roe deer is most likely to be out and about. (The Finlays' sighting, however, took place at noon.)

BAMBI?

*I*n 1923, Austrian author Felix Salten wrote a story called *Bambi: A Life in the Woods*. Anyone who has viewed the Disney cartoon adaptation of Salten's story saw Bambi as an Americanized white-tailed deer, an animal familiar to everyone in the United States. The original Bambi of Salten's story, however, was a male roe deer. That means that some people who think they've seen Nessie actually saw one of Bambi's kin taking a dip in Loch Ness. Talk about a case of mistaken identity!

THE LOCH HARBORS A SEAL

Another mammal that cryptozoologists think is sometimes mistaken for Nessie is one of the most popular residents of zoos everywhere: the seal—in particular, the harbor seal. This seal is known to inhabit the ocean surrounding the British Isles. Whereas you probably wouldn't be the least bit surprised to see a harbor seal surfing along the coast, an encounter with the same animal in the middle of Loch Ness would be totally unexpected. If you caught a distant glimpse of a seal treading water in the middle of the loch, head and neck craning above the surface as the animal checked its bearings (seals have a talent for rubbernecking, as anyone who has tossed fish treats to seals at the zoo will know), your gut instinct would tell you that the animal must be something else. Something more appropriate for Loch Ness. Such as the Loch Ness Monster. The fact of the matter, however, is that harbor seals do occasionally swim from the North Sea up to Loch Ness (via River Ness), probably to feast on salmon and other tasty fish.

The harbor seal may not be the only seal that visits the loch. Its larger cousin, the gray seal, may also visit Nessie's home once in a while. A 10-foot-long (3-m), 550-pound (250-kg) bull gray seal would certainly make quite a commotion splashing around in the water, and it could account for a sizeable hump in the water if it lolled around at the surface.

Peter Costello, the Nessie hunter who was convinced the Surgeon's photo was authentic, was certain that Nessie was a seal. Reviving an idea first suggested by Dutch zoologist A.C. Oudemans, Costello enthusiastically proposed that Nessie was a huge, long-necked seal as yet unknown to science. His roly-poly monster seal had "two or three dorsal humps, caused by the rolling up of the fat under loose folds of skin." The horns seen in the surgeon's photo were supposedly the seal's ears. Because some eyewitnesses had reported what looked like a horse's mane on Nessie's neck, Costello

Harbor seals occasionally make their way up River Ness and into Loch Ness, where they may be mistaken for Nessie.

obligingly adorned his seal with one: "What could be more appropriate for a water-horse than a mane?" If you can picture a big, fat camel with flippers instead of legs, you have a good idea of what Costello's creature looked like.

Despite Costello's energetic argument for a long-necked Nessie-seal, few people jumped aboard his bandwagon. Most had already boarded another bandwagon, and that one suited them just fine. They already knew what they were looking for. Nessie was no weird-looking seal. Nessie was something entirely different. Nessie was a huge, prehistoric, long-necked, fish-eating, four-flippered, aquatic reptile. Nessie was a plesiosaur.

PLESIOSAUR,
IF YOU PLEASE

$\mathcal{B}$efore he embarked on his fateful 1960 expedition to Loch Ness, Tim Dinsdale spent a considerable amount of time trying to determine just exactly what type of creature Nessie was. He studied all 100 eyewitness descriptions of Nessie that were presented in *More Than a Legend*, a book written by Constance White, a local resident and avid Nessie fan. As the wife of the manager of the Caledonian Canal, White was familiar with all the Nessie scuttlebutt circulating in and around Loch Ness.

DINSDALE'S PLESIOSAUR

Dinsdale found a gold mine of information in White's book. He analyzed all the eyewitness references to Nessie's size,

When most people think of the Loch Ness Monster, they picture a swan-necked plesiosaur, like this one.

shape, behavior, and the like, and when he was finished, he drew an amazing conclusion. He decided that the creature in the loch was something a bit more unusual than a loon, an otter, or a weird-looking seal. He determined that Nessie was a huge creature 40 feet (12.2 m) long, counting its 9-foot (2.7-m) neck and 10-foot (3-m) tail. It had flippers for limbs and it was, without a shadow of a doubt, one monster of a plesiosaur, a gigantic marine reptile that had supposedly become extinct along with the dinosaurs millions of years ago. Dinsdale's conclusion, which he presented in his book *Loch Ness Monster*, helped cement in the public's mind the image of a prehistoric plesiosaur plying the waters of Loch Ness.

Dinsdale realized that if Nessie was, in fact, a plesiosaur, it meant that at least one species of this magnificent reptile group managed to escape the extinction event that wiped out all of its brethren. Nessie's ancestors must have survived in the frigid polar seas surrounding the British Isles, frequented Loch Ness after the ice age glacier receded, and become land-locked when isostatic rebound isolated Loch Ness from the ocean.

Pros and Cons for the Plesiosaur

Could this unlikely series of events actually have occurred? The virtually unanimous opinion of the scientific world can be summed up in one word—*no*—for two simple reasons. First, the most recent plesiosaur fossils known are at least 65 million years old. If Nessie's ancestors had survived to the present, they should have left a fossil trail right up to modern times. They didn't, and that means that plesiosaurs are not likely to have survived. Second, fossils of prehistoric marine reptiles are usually found in sediments deposited at the bottom of warm, balmy prehistoric seas. There's no way **poikilothermic** ("cold-blooded") reptiles could survive in the icy cold water of the northern Atlantic Ocean and the North Sea and, later, in chilly Loch Ness. (The summertime surface temperature of Loch Ness rarely climbs much above 60°F [15°C], and the deeper water stays at a bone-chilling 42°F [5.5°C] year-round.)

Nessie fans, however, have answers to both of these arguments. Concerning the fossil record: The most recent fossil remains of primitive fishes known as lobe-fins, or **crossopterygians**, are a good 80 million years old. Yet in 1938, a "living fossil" lobe-fin known as the coelacanth was discovered alive and well, living in deep ocean waters off the east coast of Africa. Now, if lobe-finned coelacanths could survive all those years without leaving a fossil trace, why not plesiosaurs? So much for the fossil-trail argument.

Until recently, plesiosaur fans couldn't dispute scientists' claim that Loch Ness was too cold for a giant reptile to survive in it. The tide turned in 2006, however, when

paleontologists discovered 115 million-year-old fossils of two species of plesiosaur that inhabited the seas off ancient Australia. Why is that significant? Because 115 million years ago, the Australian tectonic plate was much closer to Antarctica than it is now, and it was smack dab in the middle of a frigid polar ocean. Apparently, some species of plesiosaur evolved the ability to maintain a warm body temperature in cold water, just like penguins, walruses, and other **homeothermic** ("warm-blooded") inhabitants of modern polar seas.

The discovery of these cold-water plesiosaur fossils, coupled with the story of the coelacanth, certainly seems to make the plesiosaur a plausible candidate for the title of Loch Ness Monster.

THE STORY OF THE BONES

Assuming that at least some Nessie sightings can't be attributed to logs, loons, and the like, it seems possible that Nessie really *is* a plesiosaur. Yet, just how closely does the beast described by eyewitnesses match the beast whose fossilized remains scientists have dug out of the earth?

It's really amazing how much information paleontologists can glean from the fossils of extinct animals. By studying the sizes, shapes, positions, and other details of the bones in fossilized skeletons, scientists can often determine how large an extinct animal grew, how it moved, what it ate, and much more. Because many good-quality plesiosaur fossil skeletons have been discovered, paleontologists have been able to put together a pretty detailed picture of the natural history of these magnificent creatures.

The Facts Just Don't Add Up

The most popular image of Nessie is that of the swan-necked plesiosaur. Could a plesiosaur actually hold its head and neck in such a position? Probably not. According to American paleontologist Michael Everhart, a number of facts suggest that Nessie could not pose that way, and that even if it could, it wouldn't want to.

Plesiosaur neck **vertebrae** (there were up to 73 of them in an elasmosaur—the extremely long-necked plesiosaur most often identified with Nessie) were strung so closely together that they barely had any wiggle room. As a result, the neck was not very flexible and was capable of very little up-and-down or sideways movement. There is no way Nessie could bend its neck into a graceful S-shaped curve. Even if it could, that pose would serve no purpose. The structure of the plesiosaur skull shows that the animal's eyes pointed in an upward direction; if Nessie assumed a swanlike pose, it would be staring up at the clouds. Furthermore, since plesiosaur eyes were probably designed for underwater vision, they wouldn't see clearly in the air. So even if it could assume a swan-neck pose, there's no way Nessie could check out the scenery above the surface or search for prey and enemies below.

Everhart presents an additional argument against the familiar head-and-neck-sticking-up-out-of-the-water pose: "Unless the laws of physics were suspended on the behalf of these extinct creatures, it would have been impossible for them to lift much more than their head above water to breathe. If you would like to prove this for yourself, try lifting a heavy pole from one end while floating in water and not touching the bottom. As you try to raise the object, your legs and lower body will also rotate toward the surface to counter-balance any weight above the water." The neck of a 40-foot, 7-ton (6,364-kg) elasmosaur would weigh almost one ton (909 kg). If Nessie tried to pose like a swan, its rump might rise out of the water like a surfacing submarine!

Another popular image of the Loch Ness Monster is that of an unidentified hump plowing through the water: A Nessie chasing down its next meal of trout or salmon. Such a scenario is certainly more exciting to a Nessie hunter than that

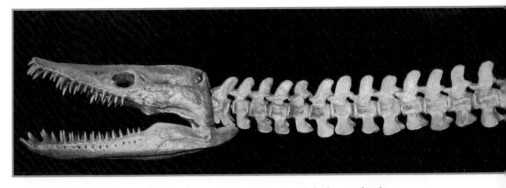

The neck vertebrae of the elasmosaur were so tightly packed together that the animal's neck would not have been flexible enough to assume a curvy, swanlike pose.

of wave interference or boat wakes, but is it likely? Probably not. The plesiosaur was not built for speed. Paleontologists believe that this reptile was an ambush-style predator that used its flippers to slowly paddle up underneath unsuspecting fish near the surface (here's where the upward-pointing eyes come into play) until it was close enough to a victim to snag it with a quick sideways jerk of the head.

Another interesting feature of the plesiosaur skull is its overall size and shape: It's downright tiny, considering the size of the rest of the body, and it has a skinny, drawn-out snout. The skull of a 40-foot elasmosaur would only be about 20 inches (50.8 cm) long, and the jaw would be a mere 7 inches (17.8 cm) wide. Since a plesiosaur's narrow, spikelike teeth were designed only to hold on to slippery prey, not slice it into smaller chunks (in the style of the great white shark), the animal had to eat its prey whole. Everhart believes that this 40-foot animal was limited to eating streamlined fish no more than 18 inches (45.7 cm) long.

This strict size limit for potential plesiosaur prey poses a particularly puzzling problem: Could this sort of reptile find enough food to survive in Loch Ness? There are actually two parts to this problem. First, we need to determine just how many Nessies would be expected to live in Loch Ness. Second, we need to know how much Nessie food lives in Loch Ness. There's no easy solution to either of these problems, but to come up with a reasonable conclusion as to the likelihood of giant elasmosaurs surviving in the loch, both of them must be addressed.

PROBLEMS, PROBLEMS

One question that this investigation has not yet dealt with is, "How many Nessies are there?" Recall that isostatic rebound after the ice age almost completely isolated Loch Ness from the North Sea. For the last 10,000 years, the loch's only natural connection to the sea has been the River Ness. This river is extremely shallow: One stretch near Inverness is only 3.3 feet (100 cm) deep.

Such shallow water is no obstacle to seals or migrating salmon, but it would probably prevent Dinsdale's ponderous plesiosaurs from traveling back and forth between Loch Ness and the sea, especially if elasmosaurs were slow-poke swimmers designed for stealth rather than speed. It would be difficult, if not impossible, for such a beast to swim up against the current all 7 miles (11.2 km) of River Ness, even if the water were deep enough (and even if there weren't a nearly 200-year-old dam near the upper end of the river, blocking the path of any modern-day monsters trying to reach the loch).

What all of this means is that Nessies, if they do indeed exist, are landlocked prisoners of Loch Ness. It also means that, unless Nessies have a life span of at least 10,000 years—a possibility too unlikely for scientists to seriously consider—they must have lived, reproduced, and died many times over in order for their kind to have survived into modern times. This is an extremely important point: If there are any Nessies at all, there must be a sizeable, reproducing population of them, and not just one or two extremely old individuals.

The Problem with Inbreeding

How large must the Nessie population be in order to survive for 10,000 years? The simplest answer to this question would be, "The bigger the population, the better." This is because a large population, which typically contains lots of unrelated individuals, is less likely to suffer the effects of **inbreeding** (the breeding of closely related individuals) than is a small population, all of whose members are usually closely related. Offspring produced by close relatives (for example, a mother and her son) often are smaller, slower growing, and more sickly than normal. Inbreeding over several generations would compound this problem and threaten the long-term survival of a Nessie population. Furthermore, small populations are more vulnerable to catastrophic events such as deadly disease outbreaks, severe weather, and whatever other curve balls Mother Nature might throw their way. There is definitely strength in numbers.

It's difficult to determine just how large a population needs to be in order to survive over the long haul. That's because a population's size is affected by its own peculiar demography—a combination of many factors, such as birth rate and death rate, that interact with each other and the environment to influence the population's growth and stability.

A 1972 *Time* magazine article claimed that a stable population of Loch Ness Monsters would contain "20 animals in a breeding herd." No one knows for sure how accurate this number is, but at least it provides us a baseline value to work with as we tangle with the plesiosaur population puzzle.

Not Enough Food

Now that we have a number to work with, it's time for the $64,000 question: Is there enough food in Loch Ness to support a minimum of 20 big, hungry fish eaters like Nessie? Probably not. A deep, skinny lake such as Loch Ness has

LET'S GET TECHNICAL: DEMOGRAPHY

$\mathcal{D}$emography is the combination of factors that influence the size and stability of a population of animals. Among the most important factors are birth rate and death rate. How many individuals are born or hatched each year, and how many die? In the case of Nessies, we just don't know.

Another factor is the overall rate of **dispersal** between populations. For Nessies, we know that the value of that factor is zero. As explained in the text, the Nessie population is landlocked, so no Nessies can get out (**emigrate**) and none can get in (**immigrate**) if, in fact, there is a population of Nessies inhabiting the ocean surrounding Scotland. (Some people think seagoing Nessies exist and may be responsible for sightings of sea serpents.) These factors are collectively known as the "BIDE factors": Birth, Immigration, Death, and Emigration.

Last but not least is the **sex ratio** of the breeding population. In our hypothetical 20-member breeding herd of Nessies, how many are males and how many are females? Ideally, there would be 10 males and 10 females, because this provides the greatest variety of parents. If the ratio is lopsided, which happens in species where only one or a few big, strong males mate with all the females, then inbreeding might come into play, as many of the offspring—that is, the next generation of breeders—would be related through their father. In the case of Nessies, we obviously have no clue as to what the sex ratio would be.

All in all, we can surmise very little about the demography of Nessies, so *Time* magazine's claim of a breeding herd of 20 animals is clearly only a guess. Furthermore, some scientists think a population size of at least 50, and perhaps as many as 500, would be needed for Nessies or any other kind of animal to survive over the long haul. If there were that many Nessies swimming around in Loch Ness, one would think they wouldn't stay unknown for long.

relatively few plants in it—compared with, say, a shallow farm pond loaded with algae, duckweed, and lily pads—because sunlight, which supplies the energy that drives the whole food chain, cannot penetrate to the bottom of the lake. Where there's no sunlight, there are no plants providing food for plant-eating herbivores (mostly little fishes and invertebrates). Without a large population of these herbivores, there are even fewer meat-eating carnivores (otters, waterbirds, and bigger fishes that eat the herbivores; Nessie would be in this category).

Technically speaking, Loch Ness is an **oligotrophic** lake: It's not very fertile or productive. Rooted plants are only found in the narrow fringe of shallow water surrounding the loch. Floating plants, such as microscopic algae, are limited to the upper reaches of the loch. Most of the deep, dark loch is devoid of plant life and therefore can produce no food for herbivores.

As one climbs the food chain, there is roughly a 90% decrease in **biomass** each step of the way. For example, 100 pounds (45 kg) of plant biomass will be converted into 10 pounds (4.5 kg) of herbivore biomass, which will in turn be converted into a single pound (450 grams) of carnivore biomass. It is therefore no surprise that oligotrophic lakes, which contain relatively little plant biomass, cannot support a whole lot of carnivore biomass. Quite a bit of carnivore biomass was packaged into just one 40-foot plesiosaur.

There are three main species of fish that a loch-bound plesiosaur would be likely to subsist on: the Atlantic salmon and its relatives, the brown trout, and charr. Most experts believe that the total biomass of landlocked trout and charr wouldn't be enough to support very many huge, voracious plesiosaurs. Two scientific studies performed in the early 1970s indicated that there is only enough biomass of resident fish to support slightly less than 17.5 tons (16,000 kg) of Loch Ness Monster mass—not even three seven-ton Nessies.

If plesiosaurs lived in Loch Ness, they would probably eat fish such as the Atlantic salmon, which pass through the loch on their way to spawning grounds at the head of streams that drain into the loch.

An additional biomass of migrating salmon, however, does enter Loch Ness from the ocean every year. The salmon migrate from the North Sea, up the shallow River Ness, into Loch Ness and then up rivers that drain into the loch, to spawn in shallow headwater streams. Could migrating salmon provide enough food to maintain a colony of Nessies? Probably not. Although no one knows for sure how many salmon migrate through Loch Ness every year, Nessie expert Adrian Shine is not convinced that there are all that many. He notes that fish counters stationed at two of the handful of rivers that Loch Ness salmon ascend every year counted less than 1,000 fish in 1975, and that was a good year for salmon.

This pessimistic outlook toward the contribution of salmon to the diet of Nessies is made even gloomier for another reason. Recall that any fish more than 18 inches (46 cm) long would be too big for even a large plesiosaur to swallow. The average length of salmon migrating through the loch is 22 inches (55.9 cm), 4 inches (10 cm) longer than the largest fish a 40-foot (12-m) elasmosaur could handle. That means that many of the migrating salmon would be too big to eat.

Maybe we can ignore migrating salmon as a food source. What if we shrunk Nessies a bit? Instead of the 40-foot length postulated by Tim Dinsdale, what if Loch Ness Monsters maxed out at only 20 feet (6.1 m)—half of which was a long, skinny neck—and weighed only, say, half a ton (455 kg), about twice as much as a bull gray seal? Then, even without migrating salmon, there should be enough fish biomass in the loch to feed 35 adult Nessies ([2 Nessies per ton] x 17.5 tons = 35 Nessies), or 20 breeding adults and a bunch of youngsters.

The Numbers Just Don't Add Up

Wait a minute: If an adult Nessie were only half as long as Dinsdale's monster, then it would only be able to eat food half as big as the 40-footer could handle, because its skull would only be half as long. If a 40-footer could only handle an 18-inch fish, then a 20-footer wouldn't be able to handle anything over 9 inches (22.9 cm) long! This means that a significant portion of the biomass of trout and charr (both of which can grow almost as big as salmon) would come in servings too big for an adult Nessie to swallow. Clearly, the amount of fish biomass available as food for 20-foot Nessies would be a lot less than the amount available for 40-footers. It's extremely unlikely that 35 smaller Nessies would find enough food to survive.

Mind you, this is all speculation, since we aren't absolutely certain how large a meal a plesiosaur could handle. It is reasonable speculation, however, based on the size and design of plesiosaur skulls, and it raises a serious question about the availability of suitably sized prey for 17.5 tons worth of plesiosaurs of any size.

Travel Time

As appealing as the plesiosaur idea is, evidence indicates that Nessies, if they do indeed exist, must be something else. Unless every honest sighting can be chalked up as a case of mistaken identity (log, bird, otter, or whatever), there's something out there that still needs explaining. Maybe a clue to the solution of this mystery can be found some place else. After all, Loch Ness isn't the only lake thought to harbor unknown water monsters. If this investigation is going to cover all the angles, it's going to have to put in a little travel time to visit other lands and other lakes . . . and other monsters.

NESSIES OF
THE NEW WORLD

och Ness isn't the only Scottish lake said to house monsters. Loch Morar, some distance southwest of Loch Ness, isn't quite as big as Loch Ness, but it's still plenty big and deep enough to house a huge lake monster or two. In fact, numerous accounts of "Morag," Nessie's counterpart in Loch Morar, have been reported over the years.

Like Nessie, Morag is commonly described as a long-necked, small-headed, multihumped creature up to 40 feet (12.2 m) long. The most celebrated human encounter with Morag reportedly took place in 1969 when two fishermen said that they fought off a monster that bumped into their fishing boat. During the course of the tussle, one of the fishermen broke a boat's oar while trying to push the beast away. Finally, the animal submerged and disappeared after one of the men shot at it with his rifle. The fishermen said that this dirty-brown creature was up to 7 feet (2.1 m) in diameter and resembled the monkfish, an oceanic, bottom-dwelling relative of sharks and rays.

Alas, the true story behind this tale surfaced some time later. The fishermen's story was a hoax—or, more precisely, a cover-up. The "fishermen" were really hunters, and the "monster" they poked and shot at was the carcass of a poached deer that they were trying to sink before coming ashore. The act the hunters put on was for the benefit of shorebound witnesses who might have reported the poachers to the authorities if the truth were to be discovered.

Reports of other Scottish lake monsters have been equally disappointing. Clearly, if this investigation is going to shed any light on this mystery, it's going to have to go international—and the best place to go is North America, which is home to a whole slew of suspected lake monsters, some of which have become almost as famous as Nessie. By comparing New World monster sightings with those of Nessie, it may be possible to find some common factors that help make sense of the whole lake monster phenomenon.

OGOPOGO

Ogopogo is a Canadian lake monster that reputedly lives in Lake Okanagan, a long, deep, skinny lake located in southern British Columbia, north of the state of Washington. Lake Okanagan is quite a bit larger than Loch Ness, measuring about 69 miles (111 km) long, 3 miles (5 km) wide, and up to 750 feet (230 m) deep. "Ogopogo" sounds like a silly name for a lake monster. Indeed, this was the name given to the beast in a song titled "The Ogopogo: The Funny Fox Trot," composed in 1924. Once this song became well-known locally, the nickname stuck. It's just as well, because the creature's real name, given to it centuries before by the

Ogopogo is one of Canada's most famous cryptids. This artist's depiction shows a creature with features similar to the Loch Ness Monster.

Native American Okanagan tribe, was a lot harder to pronounce: N'ha-a-itk.

N'ha-a-itk was not your everyday, happy-go-lucky, Nessie-type monster. N'ha-a-itk was a monster surrounded by gloom and doom. Its name meant "water demon," and its lair was said to be a cave beneath Rattlesnake Island, a craggy, uninhabited island shaped like the shell of a giant snapping turtle. This monster of the Okanagan tribe was as much supernatural as it was real: N'ha-a-itk could control the weather around the lake, whipping up deadly winds, storms, and whirlpools when it was angry. To appease the monster, the Okanagans would offer it a live animal sacrifice before venturing into the water.

Changing the monster's name reflected a change in its personality. The European settlers who colonized the region apparently lost touch with the Okanagans' legend of the irascible N'ha-a-itk and eventually transformed the beast into the inoffensive, even likeable (in a Nessie sort of way) Ogopogo.

The Many Faces of Ogopogo

Like Nessie, Ogopogo has been described in many ways, with colors ranging from black to brown to green; with a head shaped like that of a snake, cow or horse; with fins or feet; with one hump to several; and with a length of up to 70 feet (21.3 m). Whereas Nessie enthusiasts prefer to picture their monster as some sort of plesiosaur, Ogopogo fans seem to favor more of a long, serpentlike creature, whose looping coils undulate through the water as it swims. This single fact points to one very likely explanation for many Ogopogo sightings: a known resident of the area—our furry friend, the otter. It's a different species from the one at Loch Ness (the American species is the northern river otter, while the species found in Scotland is the European otter), but it's an acrobatic, sociable, follow-the-leader otter just the same.

Not all Ogopogo sightings, however, can be attributed to otters. Some sightings describe objects much too massive to be attributed to these frisky furballs. One such sighting occurred just a few years ago. Unlike most sightings, this one was accompanied by an excellent videotape, considered by many Ogopogo fans to be the best lake monster video ever recorded.

Ogopogo on Videotape

This famous Ogopogo sighting began during the calm, early-morning hours of August 9, 2004. John Casorso and his family were fast asleep aboard a 40-foot-long (12.2-m) house-boat tied to a marker buoy anchored in 70 feet (21.3 m) of water, a couple hundred yards offshore. At approximately 7:30, the family was awakened when the boat was suddenly jerked and rocked by something under the water. This motion was accompanied by a thumping sound, as if something were bumping against the houseboat's pontoons.

When the Casorsos looked out the houseboat window, they saw a dark, 15-foot-long (4.5-m), shiny, greenish-black, humped object slowly moving away. John Casorso grabbed his video camera and climbed up on deck, where he could see that there were actually several of these humps stretched along a line about 50 feet (15.2 m) long and about 100 yards (91.5 m) away. Casorso videotaped the humps as they slowly bobbed up and down in the water. The objects slowly moved in an easterly direction and then veered toward the south. A few minutes later, they slowly sank and disappeared.

"We saw what appeared to be a wave, but it didn't seem to go anywhere," John Casorso was quoted in a local newspaper as saying. "I believe it was a very large aquatic animal—maybe a reptile. It had a serpent look to it and when it moved it seemed to stretch out." It should be noted that no moving boats, a possible source of waves, were seen during the incident.

Casorso believes that this serpentlike animal may have bumped into the buoy anchor chain, which jerked at the buoy, which then jerked on the houseboat tether, which in turn jerked on the houseboat, causing it to move. The animal then bumped against the boat's pontoons as it swam under the boat, causing the thumping sound, and then surfaced and slowly moved away from the boat.

A similar hump phenomenon was videotaped at Loch Ness in 1992. A tourist visiting the famous ruins of Urquhart Castle, which is perched along the north shore of the loch, videotaped a strange sight on the water, not far from shore. It looked as if a big, black, humped creature of some sort was rolling over and over at the surface. To inexperienced land-lubbers, the tourist's video had "Nessie" written all over it. To experienced boat skippers and fishermen, however, the video was unremarkable: It was nothing more than a boat wake. Nessie hunter Henry Bauer explains: "[P]eople with some experience of actually watching at Loch Ness should have no difficulty identifying this as the single segment of a boat wake that has persisted while the other segments have died down, as happens not infrequently on calm water where the wakes roll far and endure a long time. Viewed approxi-mately side-on to the wake-section's motion, the shadow of the rolling wave can look remarkably like something solid." The giveaway that this was indeed a wave phenomenon was the repetitive nature of the rolling motion.

The humps in the Casorso video didn't exhibit the pronounced rolling behavior that was so apparent in the Urquhart video, but there are several instances where small waves can be seen rolling over the tops of the humps. Still, Mr. Casorso is convinced that what he saw was something solid, something alive—not just a weird boat wake on the surface of Lake Okanagan.

It appears that Ogopogo, like Nessie, is content to provide us with only a glimpse of itself. It's enough of a glimpse, how-ever, to pique the interest of lake monster fans everywhere.

CHAMP

Which lake monster is the most talented shape-shifter of all? Judging from all of the eyewitness reports, Ogopogo and Nessie would definitely be in the running, but first place would have to go to the champ—as in "Champ," the lake mon-ster that reputedly lives in Lake Champlain, a long, skinny, deep lake in the northeastern United States. Lake Champlain straddles the boundary between Vermont and New York, and just barely crosses the U. S. border into Canada. It is 125 miles (200 km) long, up to 14 miles (22.4 km) wide (although the southern half of the lake is quite narrow, only a mile or two wide), and up to 400 feet (121.9 m) deep.

Champ has been sighted hundreds of times since the 1800s, and each sighting is different. According to a study by skeptical cryptozoologist Joe Nickell, coauthor of *Lake Monster Mysteries*, Champ comes in a kaleidoscope of colors: black, gray, brown, green, reddish bronze, and white-bodied-and-dark-headed. It has anywhere from one to five humps or snakelike coils. It may have flippers, horns, antlers, glowing eyes, huge ears, alligator jaws, and/or a mane, and it ranges from 10 feet to more than 150 feet (3 to 46 m) in length. It has been compared to a big snake, a huge dog, a horse, a manatee, a whale, a submarine's periscope, and a telephone pole. Granted, some eyewitnesses acknowledge that what they saw might have been a waterbird, an otter, or even a big fish, but many are convinced they actually saw the monster.

The Mansi Photograph

Of all the sightings of Champ, the most famous is a 1977 encounter reported by Sandra Mansi. One July afternoon, the Mansi family's frolicking fun at the Lake Champlain beach was interrupted by an odd disturbance in the water, followed by the sudden emergence of what looked like the head, neck, and back of a large animal. Not knowing exactly what it was that they were seeing, the concerned parents brought the children out of the water and headed up the beach to the family's car, a safe distance away. The object remained in view a short time and then sank back below the surface. During the time it was visible, it never once paid any attention to all the commotion caused by the Mansis as they yelled and splashed and scrambled up the beach. In fact, the "creature" behaved more like a statue, floating in a frozen pose until it sank.

(continues on page 82)

LET'S GET TECHNICAL: EYEWITNESS TESTIMONY

One thing that we have made crystal clear is the fact that eyewitness accounts can be unreliable. Countless lake monster sightings have turned out to be anything but. Why does this happen? The following two incidents provide a clue.

Several years ago, Richard Frere, a historian and lifelong resident of the highlands surrounding Loch Ness, conspired with a friend to play a trick on motorists traveling the road that hugs the north shore of the loch. The two conspirators pulled off to the side of the road and, like all good tourists, grabbed their camera, got out of their car, and started taking pictures. At one point, as if on cue, three large boats passed by, creating a bunch of choppy, churning boat wakes. Upon seeing this, Frere and his friend started gesticulating frantically, pointed to the loch, and started taking pictures.

These antics caught the attention of passing motorists, many of whom pulled over to see what all the fuss was about. Frere and his friend told everyone that they saw a big hump out in the middle of the loch. Falling for this ruse, everyone got excited, many whipped out their own cameras, and an all-out search for Nessie began. After the choppy boat wakes dissipated, Frere talked to some of the onlookers and listened in on their conversations. A full three-quarters of the duped eyewitnesses were certain they saw long, dark humps moving through the water. Two men sharing a pair of binoculars even claimed they saw a tail and flippers! A young boy, a very good artist, quickly sketched the scene as he saw it: Along with the trees, houses, and fields in the distance, the boy sketched, smack-dab in the middle of the loch, a very good likeness of—you guessed it—a plesiosaur.

More recently, the BBC research team that performed the fruit-less sonar sweep of Loch Ness in 2003 played a bit of a trick on a group of tourists who were watching the event. The researchers, who had earlier hidden a fence post under the water, briefly shoved it above the surface when the tourists came by. The eyewitnesses were later asked to describe what they saw. Most saw a "square object," but some actually thought they saw a monster's head.

Such cases of mistaken identity can be attributed to overactive imaginations that fall victim to the power of suggestion. If a person tells you that the dark blob you see in the middle of a lake is a monster's hump, you may be inclined to agree—even though the blob is something else. If so, you will have fallen victim to the mental mistake known as **expectant attention**: When you are anxiously expecting to see something in particular (such as a monster in the middle of a lake), your mind "fills in the blanks" if what you see is unclear or indistinct, creating something (such as a monster) out of nothing (such as a blurry wave).

Then there's the related psychological phenomenon called **pareidolia**. Pareidolia is a state of mind where a vague or unclear image is perceived to be something recognizable, regardless of whether it's something you expect to see. The most famous example of pareidolia is the familiar face of the Man in the Moon. Another famous example was the Old Man in the Mountain, a rock formation on a cliff face in New Hampshire. When viewed from the right angle, the formation looked just like the profile of the face of a scraggy old man. (The Old Man's face crumbled away in 2003, but it has been immortalized in a postage stamp and the commemorative New Hampshire quarter.)

When we consider the influence of expectant attention and pareidolia, it's easy to see how a floating log turns into Champ and a flowing boat wake becomes a swimming Nessie.

(continued from page 79)

Sandra Mansi took just one photo of the object with her camera, but what a photo it was! Unlike typical Nessie photos, hers was in focus, and the object could be clearly seen. The Mansis estimated that the curvaceous "neck" of the object was a good 12 feet (3.7 m) long and reared up 6 feet (1.8 m) above the water. The humped "back" of the object extended to the right, a short distance from the base of the neck.

No doubt about it, the object in the photo was the spittin' image of an old-fashioned—but, we now know, physically impossible—swan-necked plesiosaur. Despite the clarity of the image, the "head" of the object had no detail to it: no eyes, no ears, no nose or nostrils, and no mouth. If the object in the Mansi photo couldn't be a motionless, faceless plesiosaur, there's really only one thing it could reasonably be: a twisted tree trunk, branch, or root. (A subsequent mathematical analysis of the photo shrank the height of the neck portion to about 3 feet [0.9 m], and the total length of the object—head plus neck plus back—was determined to be about 7 feet [2.1 m], an ordinary size for a hunk of driftwood.)

As Benjamin Radford, Joe Nickell's coauthor of *Lake Monster Mysteries*, put it, "The object that Mansi saw and photographed, I believe, was almost certainly a log or tree stump that happened to surface at an angle that made it difficult to identify. Sandra Mansi's own description of the object's texture supports this conclusion: 'The texture looks like bark, like crevice-y.' How could someone mistake a tree for a living creature? For anyone knowledgeable about eyewitness testimony, it's not difficult to imagine."

Why would a hunk of driftwood float up to the surface, only to submerge again a short time later? There are two likely explanations, excluding the possibility of a hoax.

On the one hand, bacteria that decompose waterlogged driftwood at the bottom of a lake produce pockets of gas within the rotting wood. If enough gas accumulates, the wood becomes buoyant and floats up to the surface. At that point, the gas escapes into the air, so the wood, like a leaky life raft, loses its buoyancy and slowly sinks back down to the bottom of the lake. The disturbance in the water that Mansi said preceded the appearance of the driftwood could have been gas bubbles that escaped from the wood as it slowly rose to the surface.

On the other hand, strong winds blowing over long, deep lakes such as Lake Champlain, Lake Okanagan, and Loch Ness sometimes produce a large underwater wave called a **seiche**. A seiche slowly sloshes back and forth from one end of the lake to the other along the **thermocline**, a boundary layer between the warm water at the top of the lake and the cold water at the bottom. As the seiche moves along, undetectable at the surface, it stirs up tree branches and other debris resting on the bottom. Sometimes this debris reaches the surface, only to sink back down to the bottom after the seiche passes.

Either one of the above phenomena could explain the emergence and subsequent sinking of the driftwood photographed by Sandra Mansi.

In May 2009, Champ became a cyberspace celebrity. An eyewitness recorded a two-minute cell phone video of an unidentified animal spotted in the shallow near-shore waters of Lake Champlain. The video was posted online on YouTube (www.youtube.com). Lake monster enthusiasts were excited because the video appears to show a large, snakelike animal slowly moving through the water. Unfortunately, the video is poor quality and the animal appears in silhouette because the sun is low in the sky behind the lake. Therefore, no details of the blurry head, neck, and back can be seen.

After analyzing the video, Benjamin Radford determined that the creature is probably a deer or moose—both of which are common in New England. A moose is more likely for two reasons. First, the animal appears to have a moose's blunt, rounded snout, as opposed to a deer's long, slender snout. Second, moose frequently take to the water in the summertime because they like to eat water plants.

The animal in the video moves very slowly, its back sometimes jerking up and down in the water, as if it is carefully walking over the slippery, uneven lake bottom. The animal's trailing wake interacts with gentle lake waves, producing an interesting interference pattern: Backlit by the sun, portions of the wake sometimes appear dark, solid, and snakelike.

Radford is suspicious of the fact that the video ends just as the animal approaches the shore. We'll never know if the animal eventually walked ashore and revealed its "en*deer*ing" qualities to the eyewitness. Nevertheless, the video is useful to this investigation because it's a good reminder that less-than-perfect viewing conditions can transform what is probably an ordinary animal into an extraordinary monster.

SOUTH BAY BESSIE

The final stop on our tour of monster lakes is a Great Lake that is as eerie as can be—well, Erie, at any rate. As in Lake Erie. Lake Erie is the shallowest of the Great Lakes, but at 240 miles (384 km) long and up to 57 miles (91 km) wide, this border lake sandwiched between the United States and Canada is many times larger than Loch Ness, and it contains more than enough fish to satisfy the appetite of the hungriest lake monster. In fact, Lake Erie is famous for its trophy-sized perch and walleye. Lake Erie, however, is also home to a less famous creature, one that might be a distant cousin of Nessie, known by the name of "South Bay Bessie."

Reports of a large, multihumped creature frequenting the shores of Lake Erie go back many years. Many of these sightings have occurred near lakeshore communities in northeastern Ohio. Typical of such sightings is one that occurred on a summer evening in 1998 at Huntington Beach, a public lakeside park in the town of Bay Village, about 10 miles (16 km) west of Cleveland. According to a report filed by cryptozoologist Ron Schaffner for the North American BioFortean Review Web site, a family visiting the park witnessed a strange sight 500 feet (152 m) offshore, just beyond one of the stone piers that jutted out from the beach. At first, the relatively calm lake surface was disturbed by a commotion of bubbles and rolling water. This disturbance then transformed into a long ripple and finally into three black humps. At first, the witnesses thought it was a tree trunk, but then it moved around in the water as if it were alive.

There are a number of clues in Schaffner's report that might explain the Huntington Beach sighting. First, the object looked, at least at one point, like a tree trunk. Driftwood is common along the Lake Erie beach, and, as previously explained, floating logs can move in the water, even against the waves, in a very lifelike fashion. It is therefore possible that the object observed was a long hunk of driftwood.

Second, the report mentioned that there were boats out on the lake at the time of the sighting. That means there were many boat wakes moving this way and that. They were undoubtedly reflecting off the piers and colliding with each other. Therefore, it's possible that what was observed was a complicated wave interference pattern. It's even possible that a large hunk of waterlogged driftwood was brought to the surface by the churning boat wakes and then caught in the middle of the interference pattern, moving around as if it were a living creature.

Finally, the report specified that the sun was in the western sky behind the object, producing a shadowy silhouette. This would make the humps look solid, even if they were nothing more than a trio of waves. Thus, the Huntington Beach phenomenon may have been nothing more than driftwood, a wave interference pattern, or a combination of the two. Then again, maybe it was Bessie.

FINAL REPORT ON NESSIE

*I*t's time to wrap things up. All the data have been collected and analyzed and a brief summary of our findings is now in order.

We've taken a good hard look at the strongest evidence supporting the existence of Nessie. Case No. 1, the classic surgeon's photo, is of historical, but not scientific, value, as it is almost certainly a hoax. It is a photo of a tiny monster model fastened to a toy submarine. Case No. 2, the Dinsdale film, was long considered to be the best evidence for the existence of Nessie, but it turned out to be a case of mistaken identity. Analysis of a video of the film showed that the object moving across Loch Ness was a fishing boat, not a monster.

The underwater photo/sonar evidence gathered by Robert Rines in 1972 (Case No. 3, the flipper photos) was

Probably the most dedicated of all Nessie hunters, Tim Dinsdale spent a quarter of a century searching for the monster. He kept searching until his death in 1987.

discredited when: (1) It was discovered that published versions of the famous photos were substantially retouched, and (2) it was determined that the sonar readings accompanying Rines's photos were most likely reflections of surface waves and the bottom of a boat, not of large animals. The eventual discovery that the "Gargoyle's head" that Rines photographed three years later (Case No. 4) was just a tree stump laying on the bottom of the loch suggests that all the objects photographed during that second venture were nothing more than bottom debris.

Case No. 5, Operation Deepscan, was another disappointment. No conclusive evidence for the existence of large beasts in Loch Ness was obtained, despite two thorough sonar sweeps of the loch. Subsequent sonar sweeps by Rines in 2001 and the BBC in 2003 were equally unproductive. Adrian Shine, probably the most experienced sonar searcher plying the waters of Loch Ness, is convinced that all really big sonar contacts are caused by underwater turbulence, such as seiches flowing deep beneath the surface. Smaller deepwater sonar hits could easily be caused by large fish (such as sturgeon) or seals. Gray seals, for example, can plunge to a depth of at least 480 feet (146 m) while hunting. Furthermore, it appears that there is nowhere near enough food in Loch Ness to support even 20 *Nessiteras rhombopteryx*, let alone 50, or 500.

What it all boils down to is this: There is no solid evidence that Nessie exists. The question remains: If Nessie is in fact nothing more than a legend, how can all the monster sightings be explained? Obviously, some have been hoaxes. Most, however, are probably honest cases of mistaken identity. Expectant attention and pareidolia have undoubtedly transformed sightings of birds, otters, logs, and waves into sightings of Nessie. Mirages have transformed more than one merganser into a monster.

It may be more than a coincidence that lakes reputedly inhabited by monsters have many features in common. Consider this: All of the monsters checked out by this investigation live in lakes that are (1) frequented by waterbirds, otters, and deer of one species or another; (2) at least partly surrounded by wooded or forested land, providing a plentiful source of tree trunks, branches, and roots; (3) long and narrow (except for 57-mile-wide Lake Erie), providing ideal conditions for boats to produce wakes that can reflect off the sides of the lakes and form large, unusual wave interference patterns when they later collide; (4) subject to atmospheric temperature inversions that can produce mirages; and (5) capable of producing underwater seiches, which can shove branches and other bottom debris up to the surface, where they may briefly and unexpectedly appear before sinking back to the bottom.

IT COULD HAPPEN TO ANYONE

It's important to bear in mind that inexperienced tourists aren't the only people who misidentify objects on Loch Ness. Tim Dinsdale, the most revered of all Nessie hunters, mistook both a tree branch and a boat for Nessie. Alex Campbell was misled by mirages and cormorants. Roy Mackal was also fooled by waterbirds. There are undoubtedly many other such cases among the ranks of Nessie hunters. Perhaps the most dramatic example of all, one that puts into perspective—and adds to the mystique of—lake monster sightings everywhere, is that of Richard Frere, the skeptic whose roadside antics fooled all those motorists driving by Loch Ness.

One calm morning, on water smooth as glass, Frere, his young daughter, and a friend ventured out onto Loch Ness in a motorboat. Out in the middle of the loch, the boat's engine sputtered and died. Realizing they were low on gas, they restarted the engine, swung the boat around, and started to race back to shore to refuel. The motor soon conked out again. While Frere was puttering with the motor, Nessie came by for a visit:

> The creature was rising out of the Loch some twenty yards [18 m] behind me. So swift had been its surfacing that its great dark hump was still concealed beneath a welter of black, cascading water. It was moving slightly away from us with a steady, powerful motion. The shock of this manifestation was so intense that the two thoughts most appropriate to

the moment—my daughter's safety and the camera next to me on a seat—had no place in my mind. There was room there only for unbearable excitement at the prospect of further and final revelation.

Then reality set in. As the big black hump slowly sank back into the water, the three amazed boaters realized they had been tricked—by a wave. The wakes created by the boat as it zipped to and fro in the middle of the loch had run into each other and formed a big standing wave. Frere continues: "I had heard about such interference effects as the true origin of a host of sightings but had never realized their unique

Does the Loch Ness Monster really exist? Does it lurk beneath the surface of mysterious Loch Ness? Will Nessie hunters ever discover this legendary beast? Only time will tell.

power to deceive. It was a subdued trio who returned to refuel. . . . It was as though we had been in the company of a celebrated magician who had just shown us the whys and wherefores of his skills."

The search for Nessie continues. The most recent noteworthy Nessie sighting occurred in May 2007, when a fellow videotaped a black object swimming across Loch Ness at about 6 mph (9.6 km per hour). Frame-by-frame analysis of the video by lake monster investigator Joe Nickell showed that the object in the video was almost certainly that furry, button-nosed Nessie impersonator, the otter.

Clearly, until rock-solid evidence in the form of an actual specimen, dead or alive, materializes—just a few bones from a decomposed carcass should suffice—the identity of the beast will remain shrouded in mystery. If that evidence fails to surface, frustrated Nessie hunters may eventually give up the search for their beloved beast. Surely, however, even if the quest for Nessie comes to an end, the Legend of the Loch Ness Monster will never die. Maybe that's how it should be.

What do you think?

GLOSSARY

Anomaly   Something odd or abnormal

Bilateral symmetry   The condition in which one side of an object is a mirror image of the other side

Biomass   The total weight of living things in a given space

Cast   An object shaped in a mold; a footprint cast is made by pouring liquid plaster into the footprint, then removing it after the plaster has hardened

Corroboration   The act of confirming or supporting

Crepuscular   Active at dawn or dusk

Crossopterygian   A primitive fish with fleshy, lobe-shaped fins

Crust   The relatively thin outermost layer of rock on the Earth's surface

Cryptid   An unknown animal that some people believe exists, even though there is insufficient evidence to prove its existence

Cryptozoology   The study of unknown or "hidden" animals

Demography   A combination of several factors that influence the size and stability of a population of animals

Dispersal   The act of scattering or moving in different directions; commonly refers to the processes of immigration and emigration

Display   The component of a sonar system (e.g., a computer screen) that records echoes detected by the system receiver

Echo   The sound wave produced by a sonar ping that reflects off an object and returns to the sonar unit

Emigrate   To move out of a region

Erosion   The gradual wearing away of surfaces through the action of wind, water, or ice

Expectant attention   A state of mind in which a person expecting to see a particular object actually thinks he or she sees that object when viewing something ambiguous or unclear

Fault   A deep crack in Earth's crust

Fauna   The animal life of a specified area or region

Forensics   The use of science and technology to investigate and establish facts in a court of law

Homeothermic   Able to maintain a stable body temperature by internal means, such as shivering or sweating; "warm-blooded." Birds and mammals are homeothermic.

Immigrate   To move into a region

Inbreeding   The mating of closely related individuals, such as mother and son

Interference   The interaction of two or more waves that collide with each other

Isostatic rebound   The rising of previously depressed portions of Earth's crust after the removal of a heavy load, such as a glacier

Lock   An enclosed part of a canal having gates for raising or lowering the level of the water

Mantle   The molten layer of Earth that lies beneath the crust

Nutritionist   A scientist who studies the effects of food and eating habits on the body

Oligotrophic   A type of lake that is unproductive or infertile; from the Greek, meaning "few foods"

Paleontologist   A scientist who studies fossils

Pareidolia   A state of mind where a vague or unclear object is perceived to be something familiar or significant

Peat   Partially decomposed plant material

Ping   The brief pulse of sound produced by a sonar transmitter

Poikilothermic   Unable to regulate body temperature by internal means, such as sweating or shivering; "cold-blooded." Reptiles, amphibians, and fishes are poikilothermic.

Range   The distance between a sonar system and the object it detects

Receiver   The component of a sonar unit that detects echoes produced by sound waves reflected off of objects in the water

Refract   To bend a ray of light as it passes from one medium to another (i.e., from warm air into cold air)

Rhomboid   A diamond-shaped geometrical figure

Seiche   An underwater wave that sometimes forms in long, deep lakes

Sex ratio   The ratio of males to females in a population of organisms

Skeptic   A person who uses science and reason, rather than wishful thinking or gut feelings, to draw a conclusion

Sonar (acronym for *sound navigation and ranging*)   A device that uses sound waves to detect underwater objects and surfaces

Standing wave   A motionless wave interference pattern

Tectonic plate   A chunk of Earth's crust that floats and moves around on the underlying layer known as the mantle

Temperature inversion   A condition in which a layer of cold, dense air lies beneath a layer of warmer, less dense air

Thermocline   A boundary layer that separates the warm upper water in a lake from the cold bottom water

Transmitter   The component of a sonar unit that emits a short pulse of sound (a "ping")

Turbulence   Wild or disorderly motion

Vertebra   One of the bones composing the backbone

Wake   The wave pattern left in water by a moving ship

BIBLIOGRAPHY

BOOKS AND ARTICLES

Bauer, Henry H. *The Enigma of Loch Ness: Making Sense of a Mystery*. Urbana, Ill.: University of Illinois Press, 1986.

Binns, Ronald. *The Loch Ness Mystery Solved*. New York: Prometheus Books, 1984.

Burt, William H. and Richard P. Grossenheider. *A Field Guide to the Mammals: Field Marks of all Species Found North of Mexico*. Boston: Houghton Mifflin, 1964.

Campbell, Steuart. *The Loch Ness Monster: The Evidence*. Edinburgh, Scotland: Birlinn., 2002.

Casey, Michael. "Add These to Kids' Plesiosaur Collections." Cleveland *Plain Dealer*, July 29, 2006.

Costello, Peter. *In Search of Lake Monsters*. New York: Coward, McCann and Geoghegan, 1974.

Dinsdale, Tim. *Loch Ness Monster*. London: Routledge and Kegan Paul, 1982.

———. *Project Water Horse*. London: Routledge and Kegan Paul, 1975.

Franklin, Ian Robert. "Evolutionary Change in Small Populations." In: *Conservation Biology: An Evolutionary/Ecological Perspective*. M.E. Soulé and B.A. Wilcox, eds. Sunderland, Mass.: Sinauer Associates, 1980.

Harrison, R.J., R.C. Hubbard, R.S. Peterson, C.E. Rice, and R.J. Schusterman. *The Behavior and Physiology of Pinnipeds*. New York: Appleton-Century-Crofts, 1968.

Heuvelmans, Bernard. "What is Cryptozoology?" *Cryptozoology*. 1 (1982): 1–12.

Mackal, Roy P. *The Monsters of Loch Ness: The First Complete Scientific Study and its Startling Conclusions*. Chicago: Swallow Press, 1976.

Martin, Robert A. *Missing Links: Evolutionary Concepts and Transitions Through Time*. Sudbury, Mass.: Jones and Bartlett Publishers, 2004.

Meffe, Gary K., and C.R. Carroll. *Principles of Conservation Biology*. Sunderland, MA: Sinauer Associates, 1994.

Nestle, Marion. "Eating Made Simple." *Scientific American*. 297 (2007): 60–69.

Nickell, Joe. "Lake Monster Lookalikes." *Skeptical Briefs*. 17 (2007): 6–7.

———. "The Loch Ness Critter." *Skeptical Inquirer*. 31 (2007): 15–16.

Odum, Eugene P. *Fundamentals of Ecology*. Philadelphia: W.B. Saunders, 1971.

Radford, Benjamin. "New Champ Lake Monster Video Surfaces." *Skeptical Inquirer*. 33(2009): 9-11.

Radford, Benjamin, and J. Nickell. *Lake Monster Mysteries: Investigating the World's Most Elusive Creatures*. Lexington: The University Press of Kentucky, 2006.

Razdan, Rikki, and A. Kielar. "Sonar and Photographic Searches for the Loch Ness Monster: A Reassessment." *Skeptical Inquirer*. 9 (1984): 147–158.

Scheider, W., and P. Wallis. "An Alternate Method of Calculating the Population Density of Monsters in Loch Ness." *Limnology and Oceanography*. 18 (1973): 343.

Sheldon, R.W., and S.R. Kerr. "The Population Density of Monsters in Loch Ness." *Limnology and Oceanography*. 17 (1972): 796–798.

Shine, Adrian. "The Loch Ness Mystery Solved." *Cryptozoology*. 4 (1984): 83–86.

Tarbuck, Edward J., and F.K. Lutgens. *Earth: An Introduction to Physical Geology*. Upper Saddle River, NJ: Prentice Hall, 1996.

WEB SITES

Bauer, Henry H. "The Case for the Loch Ness 'Monster': The Scientific Evidence." *Journal of Scientific Exploration* 16, no. 2

(2002): 225–246. Available online. URL: http://www.henry-hbauer.homestead.com/16.2_bauer.pdf. Accessed October 5, 2009.

———. "Common Knowledge about the Loch Ness Monster: Television, Videos and Films." *Journal of Scientific Exploration* 16, no. 3 (2002): 455–477. Available online. URL: http://www.henryhbauer.homestead.com/16.3_bauer.pdf. Accessed October 5, 2009.

BBC News. "BBC 'Proves' Nessie Does Not Exist," July 27, 2003. Available online. URL: http://news.bbc.co.uk/2/hi/science/nature/3096839.stm. Accessed October 5, 2009.

Celtic Network. "Kelpies." Available online. URL: http://www.celticnetwork.com/culture/mythology/kelpie.html. Accessed October 5, 2009.

Hainey, Raymond. "Biggest Highland Earthquake in 20 Years." Available online. URL: http://news.scotsman.com/ukearthquakes/Biggest-Highland-earthquake-in-20.2685801.jp. Accessed October 5, 2009.

Harmsworth, Tony. "Movie Film and Video Evidence." Available online. URL: http://www.loch-ness.org/filmandvideo.html. Accessed October 5, 2009.

———. "Other Lochs and Lakes." Available online. URL: http://www.loch-ness.org/otherlochsandlakes.html#morar. Accessed October 5, 2009.

———. "Sonar Contacts." Available online. URL: http://www.loch-ness.org/sonar.html. Accessed on October 5, 2009.

———. "The Underwater Photographic Evidence." Available online. URL: http://www.loch-ness.org/underwaterpictures.html. Accessed October 5, 2009.

Legend of Nessie. "A Geological View of Loch Ness and Area." Available online. URL: http://www.nessie.co.uk/htm/about_loch_ness/nessgeo.html. Accessed October 5, 2009.

Niednagel, Jordan. "Ogopogo Caught on Tape." Available online. URL: http://www.trueauthority.com/explorer/explorer_november2004.htm. Accessed October 5, 2009.

Radford, Benjamin. "Lake Champlain Monster," April 2004. Available online. URL: http://www.forteantimes.com/features/

articles/157/lake_champlain_monster.html. Accessed October 5, 2009.

Raynor, Dick. "A Day, and a Man, Remembered." Available online. URL: http://lochnessinvestigation.org/Remembered.html. Accessed October 5, 2009.

———. "The River Ness: From Loch Ness to the Sea." Available online. URL: http://www.lochnessinvestigation.com/riverness journey.html.. Accessed October 5, 2009.

Rines, Robert H., J.C. Rines, J.P. Fish, H.A. Carr, J. Archer, and A. Janerico. "Preliminary Results of the Search for Mid-Water Objects in Loch Ness Using a Chirp Side-Scan Sonar 'Acoustic Net' Technique." *Hydrographic Journal* 102, October 2001. Available online. URL: http://www.hydrographicsociety.org/Articles/journal/2001/102-2.htm. Accessed October 5, 2009.

Schaffner, Ron. "South Bay Bessie: A Continuing Investigation Into an Alleged Great Lakes Serpent." *North American Bio-Fortean Review* 1, no. 1 (April 1999). Available online. URL: http://www.strangeark.com/nabr/NABR1.pdf. Accessed October 5, 2009.

Shine, Adrian J. "Loch Ness Timeline." Loch Ness & Morar Project. Available online. URL: http://www.lochnessproject.org/adrian_shine_archiveroom/loch_ness_archive_timeline.htm. Accessed October 5, 2009.

——— and D.S. Martin. "Loch Ness Habitats Observed by Sonar and Underwater Television." Loch Ness & Morar Project. Available online. URL: http://www.lochnessproject.org/ADRIAN_SHINE_ARCHIVEROOM/papershtml/loch_ness_scottish_naturalist.HTM. Accessed October 5, 2009.

"Strange Sighting on Lake Champlain in Burlington, Vermont." Available online. URL: http://www.youtube.com/watch?v=YT49LQMxthg. Accessed October 5, 2009.

Time. "Science: Myth or Monster?" (November 20, 1972). Available online. URL: http://www.time.com/time/magazine/article/0,9171,712206,00.html. Accessed October 5, 2009.

FURTHER RESOURCES

BOOKS/VIDEOS

Ellis, Richard. *Monsters of the Sea*. Guilford, Conn: Lyons Press, 2004.

———. *Sea Dragons: Predators of the Prehistoric Oceans*. Lawrence: University Press of Kansas, 2003.

Everhart, Mike. *Sea Monsters: Prehistoric Creatures of the Deep*. Washington, D.C.: National Geographic Press, 2007.

In Search of History: The Loch Ness Monster. A&E Television Networks, 1998.

San Souci, Robert D. *The Loch Ness Monster*. San Diego: Greenhaven Press, 1989.

Streissguth, Thomas. *The Loch Ness Monster*. San Diego: Lucent Books, 2002.

WEB SITES

Champ of Lake Champlain
http://unmuseum.mus.pa.us/champ.htm
Provides a good overview of the Champ phenomenon and discusses the possibility that Champ might be a primitive type of whale.

Loch Ness Monster
http://www.crystalinks.com/loch_ness.html
Presents a detailed overview of Loch Ness and the evidence for its famous inhabitant, Nessie.

Nessie Caught on Tape? You Decide
http://www.msnbc.msn.com/id/18970301/
Contains footage of the May 2007 Nessie videotape; skeptic Joe Nickell determined the animal in the video to be an otter.

Ogopogo, Canadian Lake Monster
http://www.strangemag.com/ogopogo.html
Provides a good introduction to Ogopogo and includes the lyrics to the song "The Ogopogo: The Funny Foxtrot."

Plesiosaur Directory
http://www.plesiosauria.com/index.html
An information-packed Web site that contains information about the anatomy, classification, and evolution of plesiosaurs.

Sea Monster Dates Back to Dinosaur Era
http://www.msnbc.msn.com/id/13753060/
Describes *Umoonasaurus*, one of the species of cold-water plesiosaurs whose fossils were recently found in Australia.

PICTURE CREDITS

Page:
10: J. Friedrich Bertuch
12: © AP Images
13: © Graeme Cornwallis/ Lonely Planet Images
16: © Infobase Publishing
20: © Topham/The Image Works
21: © Mary Evans Picture Library/ The Image Works
25: © AP Images
36: © Fortean/Topham/The Image Works
40: © AP Images
42: © AP Images
44: © Popperfoto/Getty Images
48: © Fortean/Topham/The Image Works
52: © Debra James/ Shutterstock
55: © Laurie Campbell/Photo Researchers, Inc.
56: © AP Images
59: © Sally Scott/Shutterstock
61: Dmitry Mitrchel
65: Mike Everhart, Oceans of Kansas Paleontology
70: © J. Helgason/ Shutterstock
75: © Topham/The Image Works
87: © Fortean/ Topham/ The Image Works
90: © Steven Beaumont/ Shutterstock

INDEX

ABOUT THE AUTHOR

RICK EMMER is a substitute science and math teacher for the Avon Lake City School District in northeast Ohio. He was previously an aquarist at the Cleveland Aquarium and a zoo keeper at the Cleveland Metroparks Zoo. He has a bachelor's degree in biology from Mount Union College and a master's degree in biology from John Carroll University. He was a member of the International Society of Cryptozoology for several years. Emmer lives with his family in Bay Village, Ohio, smack dab in the middle of Cryptid Country, with the lair of the Lake Erie Monster to the north and the hideout of the Grassman, Ohio's Bigfoot, to the south.